# In John Updike's Room

New and Selected Poems

POETRY BOOKS
*Waiting for the Barbarians*
*The Barbarian File*
*The Upper Hand*
*An Ocean of Whispers*
*Postcards Home: Poems New and Selected*
*Missing Persons*
*Remembering Mr. Fox*
*Crossing the Salt Flats*

POETRY CHAPBOOKS
*Depth of Meaning*
*Seven Love Poems*
*Closings*

CRITICAL BOOK
*Beyond the Labyrinth: A Study of Edwin Muir's Poetry*

# In John Updike's Room

CHRISTOPHER WISEMAN

New and Selected Poems

The Porcupine's Quill

Library and Archives Canada Cataloguing in Publication

Wiseman, Christopher, date
In John Updike's room : new and selected poems / Christopher Wiseman.

ISBN-13: 978-0-88984-273-1.--
ISBN-10: 0-88984-273-6

I. Title.

PS8595.I816 2005      C811'.54      C2005-901466-0

Published by The Porcupine's Quill, 68 Main St, Erin, Ontario NOB 1TO.
http://www.sentex.net/~pql

Readied for the press by John Metcalf.
Copy edited by Doris Cowan.

Represented in Canada by the Literary Press Group.
Trade orders are available from University of Toronto Press.

We acknowledge the support of the Ontario Arts Council and the Canada
Council for the Arts for our publishing program. The financial support of the
Government of Canada through the Book Publishing Industry Development
Program is also gratefully acknowledged.  Thanks, also, to the Government
of Ontario through the Ontario Media Development Corporation's Ontario
Book Initiative.

 Canada Council for the Arts   Conseil des Arts du Canada

 Canadä

 ONTARIO ARTS COUNCIL
CONSEIL DES ARTS DE L'ONTARIO

This book is dedicated to my mother
and my granddaughter

Winifred Agnes 1906–2001

Rachel Winifred 2000 –

CONTENTS

# New Poems

There's a woman, dead at eighty-seven, who's left
Half a million pounds to the lifeboat station
In the small village of Wells-next-the-Sea in Norfolk
Because that boat, in 1942,
Went out and fought the heavy seas for hours
To save her fiancé who'd ditched his Lancaster
Bomber in the North Sea — they couldn't find him —
And after that, though very deaf since birth,
She learned to fly, ending up ferrying
Bombers from their factories to their bases
Until the war was over, lived frugally (it says),
Lived in self-containment, quietly, saying
Occasionally to people that she regretted
Not having children but the only man
Who could have fulfilled (she said) that one wish
Had been lost at sea, and nobody knew more
As her long life moved, about the village lifeboat,
The bomber, anything of that time when
Life had almost opened up for her
And was just waiting to drench her with its gifts,
Like the gift she's now amazed the village with,
Or what it took away when that huge sea
One day gulped down her chance to live the way
She hoped, the way, for God's sake, she'd hoped for,
Pulled from her all her babies and her youth,
All love, no love for sixty silent years,
Living frugally (it says), alone,
And perhaps I wish I hadn't read her story,
Hidden in the place where odd things happen,
Often funny, back page of the paper,
Down at the bottom, called 'Social Studies'.

If I had to choose the silliest, saddest,
Most unlikely person to pull out
Of my by now pretty well-stocked memory,

It would have to be this one, Monty, someone
I only saw three or four times in my life
When I was thirteen or fourteen (which could

Explain, those skittish teenage years, why he's
Still with me, for there was wonder in him
For us at that odd age when everything

Sticks and stores itself) and here he comes,
Dripping, rising inconsequentially
From some dark depth in my hoping-for-more

Head, and I have to let him do a last trick.
He'll be long dead now, will Monty, buried
Somewhere in Scotland where I saw him when

We were pulled north for holidays and spent
Most days in the outdoor pool, unheated
Sea-water, temperature — fifty-six

To sixty degrees — chalked daily on a blackboard,
And we needed cocoa from the woman
In the tiny corner kiosk after swimming,

Teeth clattering with cold and teenage nonsense.
Monty wore a black wool bathing costume
With shoulder straps, which, when wet, showed all

Too clearly his very ample cock and balls
Which we couldn't help staring at, uncertain,
Just discovering how our smaller ones worked.

Balding, shouted on by swimmers and all
Those sitting around, he commandeered the deck
Under the diving boards, glorying in all

The attention, thinking himself a hero, never
Dreaming once that we were laughing at him.
He'd wave his towel round his head and laugh back.

He did tricks, did Monty. Like a big loud child.
He had four, I think, and he'd announce them, shouting
In Glaswegian. They were jumps, forward

Or backward, into the pool, arms waving,
Pulling faces, yelling, making splashes.
I can only remember the Dying Duck (flapping

And quacking in mid-air) and his Rin-tin-tin,
Which involved growling, a bark, and a doggie-paddle.
People would shake his hand, pass him his towel,

And he'd giggle and preen and promise new tricks soon.
Who in hell was he? He ignored us kids,
And my father told us that he wasn't quite right,

But his boisterous self-congratulation, his confidence,
Half impressed that shy hormonal me,
And when I went back there quite recently,

My eyes went directly to his empty place,
Still not knowing why he mattered, why
It was that our first questions on getting there

Each day, running down the beach, trunks rolled
In white towels, sixpences hidden for cocoa
Later on, were always *How cold's the water?*

And then, our heads turning, *Is Monty there?*

17

*... readying myself for death with tears.*
    — John Updike,
      'Marine Hotel, North Berwick, Scotland, May 1998'

I'm in your room — I asked them at Reception;
Sea-facing windows, big TV — where you sat
Watching *High Society,* alone,
Trying to dry your best golf clothes, and crying

For Bing, for the lost brightness of Grace, for 'True
Love', blue and perfect, and for Frank, just dead.
Outside, along the links, cold rain had lashed you,
Caddies mocked, and here you pondered darkness.

I'm sorry it turned that way for you, though such
Days become less rare, and I know why
You cried, for apart from mourning that blue Hollywood
It's the way Grace's young crossed arms reach high

For the kiss with a soft special tenderness
Which makes the loss more cruel. But no,
Not now, you won't get me, not here. The skies
Outside are clear, and you won't do it to me.

This town is where I spent my summers before
Grace sang, running through early adolescence,
Past this hotel, toward the pool and harbour,
Bright and bursting with freedom and speed, no sense

Of what appalled you about the soul of this country
And turned your room to a private Gethsemane.
I burned brown here, swam far out in that sea,
Stole golf balls, kissed girls, and I smile at who

I was. Sure I've watched *High Society* and grieved,
But far from here where now the sun throws shadows
Of that boy racing the summers for his life.
But damn you, John, something's prickling my eyes,

That thing you knew here, and darkness is coming fast.

It's just another Latin American dance these days,
For competition or pleasure, a standard, but then,
In the mid-1920s, it was sin itself,
Corrupt and corrupting, forbidden in any place

That called itself respectable. So it is that they,
My daughter-of-a-vicar mother and my son-
of-a-respectable-local-headmaster father, were the very
Last you'd expect, looking back at it, to do what they

Did at that final College ball at Durham, and, more,
To have rehearsed it, obviously, so many times.
It came, after all, that rhythmic, bending dance of sex,
From the seedy Buenos Aires waterfront, from whore

And sailor, bar and bordello, at the very end
Of the 19th century, becoming a slithery unstoppable
Pandemic, spreading underground so quickly that they
Couldn't catch it or even slow it, so how to comprehend

This particular pair, under the shadow of the cathedral
At Durham, the women students closely chaperoned …
Well, her sister was there and told me about the way my father,
Top oarsman of the College boat, and known by all

As a bit dashing, my aunt's word, slipped the bandleader five bob
And then, as that forbidden music started, grabbed my mother,
Also well known as the best tennis player they had there,
And their friends, the other dancers, did a perfect rehearsed job

Of circling them, keeping the horrified chaperones away,
And to great roars of approval, respectability
Forgotten, they let the dangerous tango have its head,
Sensual, preening, sexy, a wild magic day

I'd give anything to have been able to see.
Applause thundered. Harshly disapproving words
Were spoken to the band and the perspiring couple,
But they still got their degrees, then wed, then they had me,

Though all my life, through war and peace, everything, I never
Once saw them act that way. Never once saw them dance,
Come to that. I think of how shocking that tango was,
Most never having seen it danced, the moral weather

Low and thick at Durham, those grey and ancient schools.
What they did was revolution, from whorehouse to saintly
Walls in thirty years. They did what people just whispered about.
How glad I am they danced clear through the rules!

Fires, lust and daring! My dear lost fools!

(Manchester, England, 1951)

Just fifteen, we'd had to lie to get in there.
The sprung floor shook us at our small back table
As the dancers pranced out for the jitterbug,
Cocky, haughty, bright skirts snapping round,
Whipping, frothing, wide and high, their faces
Serious, without expression. I heard
Judy gasp when right in front of us
One woman was pulled hard through her partner's
Legs, skimming the floor, then cartwheeled high and oh
So slowly up over his shoulder that
She stopped there, upside down, for long seconds,
Her skirt down over their faces, her stocking-tops
And startling white thighs, her lacy knickers,
Everything she had on show as we watched,
Excited, until he lowered her, soft
As a petal to the floor, chewing his gum.
We were out of our minds, the four of us,
Straight from church dances, jiving forbidden,
Our sex games furtive at parties or in cinemas,
Not prepared for things like this, aroused.
We were out of place, sheltered, irrelevant.

The Levenshulme Palais. I drove past last
Year and it's still there — now the Palace Night Club.
Judy, Brenda, Mike and I stayed friends
After that night, though nothing was quite the same,
Then drifted apart, our own lives taking us.
But those dancers, are they still there? I'd like
To think that some of them, now old, still go there,
Are still friends, recalling their teens and twenties,
All those gum-chewing, drinking, smoking, Stockport
Road toughies at play, who'd made us face ourselves
And know how young we were, how far we had
To go, to grow up, to understand enjoyment.
I want them to be there, toasting their lives.

The Palais. Forbidden to us — its reputation.
I still remember faces, attitudes,
As for one wild, hot and noisy night those men
In suits and their willing, flying, high-heeled women
Made us go along with them to new places,
As down and through and up and over, taunting,
Strutting, whirling, they threw at the dull world
And at our young and unfulfilled grey lives,
Everything they had, defiant, loose,
Work and wars and modesties forgotten,
Rejoicing at their weekend place of worship,
Watched by four young kids, their blood on fire,
Who for long amazing hours just sat
Still and watched them fly like crazy angels.

Square table, square white tablecloth,
a straight partition behind, a wall
with one oblong colourless picture —
it's a pale still architecture
I'm looking at, though holding, it's true,
your barely moving head and shoulders.
A remarkable stability. Comfortable.
Behind me the bustle, voices, feet,
movement aplenty, all the whirling
shapes we're used to, but I'm caught
in a square of lines, and it's easy
to settle for, this consoling framework
fitting so easily together, not bothering
eyes or mind, but then you, you would, you
cross your legs under the square table,
and, pushing the frame so easily aside,
your leg, at least to the knee, out of
the square white hanging tablecloth,
so curved and shapely as any imagined
woman's leg could ever possibly be,
slowly swings at its complete ease,
and see, too, the delicate, coloured
high-heeled shoe, freed at the heel,
dangling loosely from your toes
and I can even read the name inside it
as your leg becomes a silent metronome
destroying all the symmetry, everything,
and if anyone thinks I am in any way
stirred and shaken by this look-don't-touch
taunting echo of so much, so many,
then they could be right, and even if,
perchance, *la donna* here turns out to be *mobile*
and this never happens again, then I
still have it all now, colour and shape,
in the surprisingly full, and, I have to admit,

favourite part of my mind, which holds
much of how I've been distracted away
from the obvious, from the straight narrow
lines of a too easy pushing onwards, and we talk
about, what else, to your shoe's rhythm,
the art of ending lines in poems
and what strong effects that can have.

THE PLACE LEFT BEHIND

(for Donald Justice, d. 2004)

> *Now alone that saddest of all instruments*
> *tells its touching tale*
> — Trollope, *The Warden*

Look. The place left behind sits in a pale sun.
The music huts are empty, musicians gone

Back to Europe, Japan. Now silence insists,
But what a flutter when they scrambled on buses,

Loading instruments, protecting expensive tuxes,
Concert gowns, new photographs and tapes.

And Heidi-Marie is gone, taking her cello,
She who would sit with me to help my slow

German translations, whose sorrowing strings, deep
And strangely knowing, brought tears not just to me.

Bright her braided hair! Heidi-Marie,
Brimming over with future, with serious joy,

Wrist bandaged and aflame from all she brings
With each passionate vibrato to those tough strings.

O well met! A surprise gift, she, in this place,
A memory, a resonance, a face

I already feel I shall move towards, precious
In these ungood days of too many dear lost faces.

Now that saddest of instruments tells its tales elsewhere,
Makes others, too, feel beyond themselves. So fair

She was! The deep echoes! The way I care!

He's there, yes with Hardy, Larkin, Heaney,
Other hero writers I would kill
To write half as well as, know I never
Will, but they make me try to. I got their
Cards at the National Portrait Gallery in London
While his is an action photograph by one
Of the press photographers sitting to the side
Of his goal, black and white, from 1952,
With behind him the big covered main stand,
Packed that day with some of the 75,000
There, tiny pale dots, no features, and I
Am one of those dots, for I was there that day,
Young, hero-worshipping, before I'd ever
Heard of Hardy, never mind Larkin or Heaney,
Up there with my father, towards the back.
He had poetry.

       Look at him here, up high
To his right, arm extended, the ball, tipped
Over the bar, up behind him, his other green-jerseyed
Arm stretched down behind him, legs flexed at the knees,
Long fair hair floating. How hard to avoid
Sports journalese to give the picture — all those
Over-used adjectives given to the very top stars —
But he looks loose and yet poised like a ballet dancer,
Or, say, caught in air between two trapezes,
A fluid cat, no angles, and even without
Seeing his face, his hair, I'd know right away
Who it was, from all the hundreds I have seen,
From this one leap. Gracefully sublime, something
Like that, the fine contours of all his movements,
And I could get teary just watching him come out
To pluck a high cross from the air above
Straining heads. Artistic. Poetry.
Nobody in Britain had seen goalkeeping like it.
Even my quiet father — *Just incredible!*

Not a bad hero, I now think, no, assert,
For a boy and his much-grown-up self to have.
A German paratrooper, in prison-camp
Near Manchester most of the war, he signed
In 1949, a bit too soon
For the then ex-soldier crowds who jeered at first,
Made Nazi salutes, protested outside the ground,
Forty thousand of them, until his excellence, his grace,
Turned him into part of Manchester City,
Changed him from Bernd Trautmann to 'our Bert'
(2004 he was given an OBE by the Queen
For services to Anglo-German relations,
Fifty years too late but at last an honour).

Best in Britain by far, and Europe too —
Bert and Lev Yashin of the Soviet Union.
Nobody else came close. A goalie myself,
I tried to imitate him, tried to be
As good — and I wasn't all that bad, to be honest —
Tried to be him, rode my bike to see
His house, the road where his young son was run
Over and killed, got his autograph,
Read his ghost-written autobiography
Until I knew the text almost by heart
As I know Larkin — to make that point again —
Watched in unashamed tears, age twenty,
At Wembley Stadium in 1956
As he played for twenty minutes with a broken neck
And City won — they guessed the crowd in the streets
At a hundred thousand when they brought the Cup home,
And he was named Footballer of the Year —
Just got, last year, another autograph,
He in his eighties, I jumping up in the sixties,
*For Chris, with best wishes, Bert Trautmann,* for
He's still around, my boyhood hero, looking

Good, living in Spain (his neck still hurts in the cold)
Brought back to Manchester from time to time
By the club to open a stand, sign photos and such.

He refused, though, did Bert, disappointing me,
To sign *From one old goalie to another,*
But now, thinking on, he was dead right not to,
For that would have altered our relationship,
Reduced him, made me too big, when he lives,
Always has and will, as heroes must, above me,
Deftly dealing with shots which would stagger me,
Catching what, helpless, I could only claw at,
Or, more likely than not, give up on, sadly,
Well beaten, though I'm exactly his height.
My limitations!

       I have Larkin's and Heaney's
Autographs too, but I'd give them up before his,
For look along this ledge at all of them
And see how he makes them, my great hero writers,
Look so ordinary — static, crumpled, dull
Specimens in their chairs, each lacking leap,
Never knowing, posed in their portrait clothes,
All wearing ties, the marvelling approval
Of seventy-five thousand roaring throats, which still
Deafens my head and makes my blood pump hard.
How lucky — I smile but mean it — they are to be
There with him in this gallery of mine.

*Ein Heldenleben.* He's been so much a part
Of the person I've become, oh God he has,
And there I am, with all the others, unfocused,
My face tiny, insignificant, watching him.

GRANDDAUGHTER, FIRST MEETING
(for Rachel)

Not the best place for our meeting, this,
New one, Calgary airport at Christmas,
But here we are at last, alone, I feel

For just a minute, as I watch your eyes
Wondering at it all, admire your calm,
Your whole hand round my finger, gripping hard,

A quietness in your face, entirely you.
You were born early and I was in Montana
Having to tell someone and ended up

Toasting you with a waitress in a family
Restaurant, feeling lost and a bit silly.
I never saw either grandfather, missed

Them by years, though I often stand by graves,
Have nothing of one, two postcards of the other,
Handed down. I want to last longer,

A few more years, so you can say you knew me,
Remember me somehow, though you won't ever
Recall this gripping of my finger today.

Such fierce holding! Little girl, don't let
Me go. I'm not steady. But now, since that day,
I feel you round my finger like a ring.

A wall of silence. Nobody will talk
About it, what you did, not those who played
With you (some dead too), the Society,
Still flourishing, dedicated to the band,
Its newsletter full of reminiscences,
Even an interview with your then young daughter.

Tall, ex-Guardsman straight, big smile, flashing
Wicked eyes. I talked a bit with you
Over beer in the Porcupine, between your sets,
Across Great Newport Street from the basement club
Now marked with a blue plaque as important
For London, for Britain, for those who once played there.

What a front line — Colyer, Wheeler and you —
Your horn loud and full, sad, boisterous, alive,
Our own Kid Ory, marches, blues, ragtime,
And you winked at the girls, who always moved for you,
Danced, hot, whirling their skirts up so you could see.
You sang, too, a bit like Armstrong but quite yourself —

*Tout de moi, pourquoi ne prends tout de moi?*
And we roared you on, just wanting all of you.
But, as I said, they all still keep it quiet,
Perhaps not just because of how you did it —
Gasoline over yourself and matches — but
That you had to do it twice, still half alive

After the first attempt. Why immolation,
For God's sake, Mac? I've heard your wife had cancer,
That you thought rock was making you obsolete,
Your talent unwanted, that you couldn't get gigs.
So will it all be kept muted, or, perhaps,
Be dealt with by cheap evasions, and puns,

Uneasy jokes, I mean, like saying your eyes
Flashed sparks too often, or that your horn made
*le jazz hot*? That's one way, and I'll have to do
It here. But first a toast, with my sad eyes —
Long cool pints, Mac, for all the years you've missed.
You lived so brightly life just burned you out.

GIVINGS AND TAKINGS AS WE AGE
(for Don Coles)

There are times when I come close but I rarely best you —
Poems, cities, gardens, your ear so fine
You catch all my nuances when I test you

On books, past lovelinesses, what possessed you
To turn down some girl in those days of softness and wine.
There are times I come quite close but rarely best you

With your poignant or joyful anecdotes, though, lest you
Forget, I have some too which we both think fine,
And you catch all my nuances when I test you,

Shyly or braggartly, about something, and you
Respond well as our ageing memories entwine.
Such times we're close but still I rarely best you.

Soccer, the war, how Germans braid hair, so fast you
Pick it up. Poems too, both dismal and sublime.
You catch all my nuances when I test you,

And add more, wisely chosen, well confessed. You
Quote back, trump me with some new-to-me Fräulein,
And there are times I've come close but rarely best you,
Though I never say how much I've smiled and blessed you.

AT THE HOSPICE

## 1. Check-in Time

Here's where you have to leave your stuff, all those
Things you've always had to deal with, for,
Hard to believe, you'll never (well, who knows,
Miracles happen) need them any more —
Clothes, music, work, shopping, movies, car,
Sex, restaurants, bills, holidays, books
Of the serious kind, oh all the things we are
Governed by. Gone now. And when somebody looks
In, they'll see you in a quiet room, in bed
Or a soft chair, busy only with family
And close friends, it's as simple now as that
And more than enough to try to manage. Dead
Easy, really, and a good thing, for see
Your face, now recognizing who and what.


## 2. Apologies

I called you there.
*Come and see me in the charnel house*
*if you think you can stand it.*

Your face was lined, less full,
and you apologized for the room,
the chair, for dragging me there,
for everything. You were sorry.

You asked me only one favour —
not to tell you, if I knew, how long you had.
I agreed and touched your arm.
You smiled. Then *I would have liked*
*a few more years,* you said, and I nodded
and could only say *Oh God yes. I'm sorry.*

Thirty years of friendship
And so little I knew to say. Angry
with myself, I knew I must come again
to make amends, say something better,
be of some help if I could.

And then you said, as if in some sort of unholy
collusion with me, *What a life, eh?*
And those four words, just then, just there,
to me contained the whole of *King Lear.*

TO A LOST GRANDCHILD

No stone for you, carved with your name,
But know you will be well remembered,
Tough one, clinging on for your dear
Life. You never breathed our air
Or saw our light, but I still claim

You as grandchild. I always will.
But now no funny faces, no
Games, nor my reading stories. All
Gone the jokes, the model planes, football,
Everything you and I together. I will

Miss it. You can't know how I
Am, how hopeless, emptied, reduced.
I wanted better than this worst.
That wave on your one film — your first
Hello, your terrible last goodbye.

Four silk scarves I bought for four women,
Gauzy, slippery, bright. In air they floated,
Escaping when I tried to fold them, barely
There, insubstantial in my clumsy hands.

The young ones, daughters-in-law, different,
Open theirs — one a bit puzzled, uncertain,
Smiling, not saying much; the other straight
Away hugging me, talking about how

It would go with some favourite blouse. After
Watching them, my wife opens hers, smiling
At me, not saying much at all, but there's some
Deep thing in her eyes, and she holds it more

Familiarly, with her wrists, not hands,
Allows the soft folds of scarlet and blue
To float downwards, to open like a flower,
And I knew she would, for that's exactly what

My mother had done, her ninety-year-old wrists
Displaying it, crying a little, the one
Who taught me how to give, how to withhold.
So many gifts in a life like hers, but fewer

In the long widowhood. And now she's gone,
Ashes light in the air, mild and light.
Gone the old wrists, the delight, the kind face,
But somehow gifts which I can hardly fold,

My other women holding on to them,
Drape me now, and I know that something goes on
And will continue. May all her family
Live so well, though they weren't there to see

Her hold her arms out for the special thing.

Kayenta, Arizona, left behind,
We head north for the unlikely-named Moab,
Utah, in summer heat, and suddenly
We're in a movie set. Unsettling, this,
As it's familiar ever since I saw
*Stagecoach* as a kid, and then John Ford's other
Takes, loving and obsessive, of the place,
But far bigger, bright red, totally silent.
We never expected the size of it, never
Knew it was close to a hundred miles long
Right up into Utah. It stops us. It
Petrifies. We gather some red stones
For paperweights. No sound. No cars. Just us
In a world like no other ever before dreamed of,
Our little camera helpless, even our eyes
Too small to capture it, to hold the scale.
Red carpet of desert, the huge cathedral rocks,
Many remembered from the screen. All red,
Massive, they would dwarf Durham, Chartres,
Köln, Notre Dame. Parched we drink from bottles.
North, searchers, always north towards Moab,
And I speed up to crawl at eighty and ninety
And I'm whistling through my teeth, Jean tells me later,
'Around her neck she wore a yellow ribbon'
And then 'I'll take you home again, Kathleen',
Over and over, feeling pursued, threatened
Somehow by all of this, in our car that's green
Like Ireland — Ford, McLaglen, Maureen O'Hara —
An unlikely colour in such a world of red.

We emerge slowly through sheer rock canyons
To signs at last for Moab and Salt Lake City
And we see more cars stagecoaching, heading south,
As we drive into Moab, flattened, car dusted red,

And quickly we stop at the first place we see,
Drink ice water, milkshakes, and don't say much,
Then past the motel where John Wayne always stayed
To our dark room, blinds tight against the sun.

So what was it with Ford and that place, we ask
Each other, the question forced, a bit scary,
For we know, and say it, that we shall go back there,
Perhaps on a guided tour next time, with others.

Driving north, ten miles away I see it,
The Law, that hill there on the flat coast land,
A weird and massive cone. It's a surprise,
As always, but this time, after fifty years,

It challenges me, tries to shrink my life,
Reminds me that I never, now, can seem
To just mess around, feel free to do what I want.
Young, I climbed it nearly every day,

Year after year, fit and lean, with friends
Or by myself, sitting at the very top
Under the arch of a long-dead whale's jawbones,
And from there, from then, I could see much more

Than now — not just down the Forth to Edinburgh,
Across to Fife, out to the Bass and the Isle of May,
But more of my life and its long stretches ahead,
Where we were going, our family, together,

That day, next week, next year. It was simple when
There was no real past to ponder. Today I look but don't
See much except for the dead weight of its stone.
My mother's young voice — *Come straight back down, Chris.*

*Sometimes I think you'll stay up there all your life.*

They move through the winter days,
Doughty, well bundled up. They
Must be in their eighties, these two,
But never fail to appear. The grey
Weather wraps them and the very few
Others out and about. At three
The same bench, cups, a flask of tea.

Wind rattles my old hotel window
As I watch them talking below
And I wonder what it is they can say
So calmly, what it is they know
That bears repeating every day.
The past, is it? Their children? I doubt
They'd dare let thoughts of future out,

And the present's just the same each day.
Should I go join them? No. Not the way
They seem simpler than I, more content
With things, less eagerly off and away
For excitement, rolling in the hay,
So to speak. They're better with how it went
Than I, the years disappearing, the portent

Of what's coming, I mean. They sit on
Through the December afternoon,
Happy, I have to think, some peace made,
Too firmly settled for even one
Of them to feel disturbed, betrayed
By what they might, once, have been,
Have made of it all with more prizes won,

As I do here, a lonely father and son.

HOT AND FAST, WITH ECHOES
(for Micheline Maylor)

> *But, though we cannot make our sun*
> *Stand still, yet we will make him run.*
> — Andrew Marvell

You speed towards the birth, your first,
big as a sedan, that last year's sleekness
overtaken by it, and looking at us
now — your belly, serious conversation,
sobriety on the table between coffee cups —
nobody would guess about last summer,
that afternoon starting right here. It was like this.
Iced coffee, so hot Calgary is,
you with bare legs and floaty miniskirt
planning for a year away,
and you are bright and giddy this day
and point to the street and say come
on, it's time for you to drive it,
its sky-blue of my lifelong soccer team,
top down, leather seats, wood dash,
your Triumph TR6 there, shining,
waiting, but I won't drive, it would be
somehow too intimate, too rich and big
a thing for me to do, so I slide
into the other seat, you at the wheel
putting your dark glasses on, checking
those round dials, and I can't believe it,
how fast the years have raced since I
borrowed my friend Tony Long's
dark green TR2 at Cambridge, going
to collect my then woman from her college,
sailing up King's Parade in second, revs high
to draw attention, for I was young,
and this could be that same amazing car
as you start it up and I buckle in

and stretch my legs deep into the well
until they are straight, and your slender
fingers and thumb caress and ease the choke,
massage it gently to its perfect setting
and your long legs move, sliding,
as you work the stiff long-throw clutch
and throttle and we're away now,
your hair blowing, the streaming road just
below my elbow on the door, guttural
the exhaust exciting everything in me
and I'd forgotten how narrow the TR is
as just inches away from mine your legs
rub against each other, confident,
hot, and I swear I hear their skin on skin
as you change gears — how remarkably
the world sometimes bestows its gifts —
and tweak us easily through the traffic
with a growl, a wave, a touch of power,
and my smile must be bigger than belief
and you are smiling too for it's wild
in the pulse this special summer riding
and I guess you feel this elation of mine
but can't know quite how deep it goes
with that earlier ride mixed up now
with this one, and your sunlit legs,
your skirt as high as it can go,
and I swear to all that's hot and crazy
that the sun is growing bigger all the time
and dancing as it chases us round the streets
and you're driving me, driving me
crazy with everything, with this
and all those years ago when I
was in this same seat — right-hand drive —
as I am now, and again I see you
changing gear, legs moving, and then all

of a sudden it nearly happens, me just
not thinking, thinking left years behind,
and I start to drop my left hand down
on to your thigh the way I did
in Cambridge (though then I got
laughingly excitingly tangled in her puffy
petticoats) actually raise it and move it down
but that was then, and different with her,
and I only just stop myself now, I'm
only just in time, and I think what if you
saw it start, that nothing but casual, supremely
natural movement of my hot hand,
and I guess that you know I nearly did that
as you smile and on and on we go,
today and in memory, a generous woman,
blown hair, a car alive all around me,
the sense that all at once I'm free from me
to be the self I think I never quite became
as the exhaust throbs throatily and echoes
and people stare and you suddenly speed up
and it will be over far too soon
as I yell out loud at the spinning sun
which again I swear is getting bigger
and you laugh, sliding your legs,
those soft magnets for the eyes, and I sense
in all of this not unholy exultation
a wild collusion far outside time's gripping,
feelings wide open for just this hour,
and the sun gets even hotter and I care nothing,
nothing at all, as you turn to me and smile,
that hey, hey-ho, this day and that other day
before, elected and elated, I'm riding
fast and oh so hard towards my dying.

*from* **Waiting for the Barbarians** (1971)

Check the laundry room
during the day and you'll see them,
washer and dryer, standing quietly
next to each other, a matched pair
minding their own business.
At night it's different.

It's not surprising.
Think of their frustration
standing day after day
with bare white flanks touching
each throbbing with power
but programmed separately.
No wonder they go mad
when we're not there.

Exactly what they do we don't know —
genial couplings with hoses
switches and cords;
clumsy titanic orgies —
we have never disturbed them.
All we know is that in the mornings
curious beads of moisture
stand on their gleaming sides,
the basement air is warm,
and on the floor
confused marks of castors
and a sinister trace of suds.

One night perhaps we shall creep
down and surprise them.
But now, our claim to the house less,
we go to bed earlier and earlier.

I am uneasy here
Watching this famous pair
Perform their love scene.
The fellow in the tights
Worries me most. Suspicious,
My eye goes to his crotch.
There's enough there certainly
But tied down so tightly
You'd think he was trying to hide
Some gross impediment.
And she is just as bad
In her silly gauze skirt,
Swooning, half-reluctant,
Settling like a white
Balloon on a draughty floor
To the coy shimmer of fiddles.
Imagine him in bed
With her, stripped of music
And humping her for real....
No. And that's what's wrong.

Soon it will be over
And I'll escape. Tall,
Awkward, trousers flapping,
Clumping on heavy heels,
I'll walk the dull grey streets
To my untidy flat,
My monstrously pregnant wife,
And the world I live in.

Charmed by the cute Disney appearance,
The hint of domestic dogginess
In the brown rheumy eyes, night
After night girls climb his stairs.
Perhaps they go to comfort him,
This stooping scholar with the glasses,
Perhaps to sit at wise old feet
And confess some frisky indiscretion.
No matter. Their safety is assured.
No wolf could fake this sort of tameness —
Or so they think until he slips
His leash. Then see him speeded up,
Jerking in coloured animation,
The cartoon teeth looking very sharp,
The prey in slightly comic flight,
Until, with a flourish, The End.
In the slow black and white of morning,
He lopes to his classroom full of girls.

DRACULA

The story, we feel, starts perfectly —
The brooding Transylvanian landscape,
Travellers, a storm, the quaint inn
With its Brueghel peasants, merrymaking
Forgotten and stiff with superstition,
Grouped around the scrubbed table,
The muttered rumours of strange happenings
In the old castle, low unearthly
Noises in the forest, and, worse,
Of something coming at dead of night
With a bang of shutters to the beds
Of trembling village girls, pinning
Them to stifling sheets and leaving
Two rubies livid on their necks.
Then the dazed silent village slowly
Gathering strength in the pale morning
Only to find in the baroque graveyard
Some hand has thrown the stones aside
And the musty smell of death is there.

But now what ending is possible?
Surely we are not to believe
That a six-inch crucifix
Held in pious trembling hands
Could shrivel like a spent balloon
One whose spreading shadow covered
Half of Europe? Or that a handy
Stake could drive that presence out?
This could not end with evil neatly
Piled in ashes on the floor,
A mild light beaming through the forest
And peasants dancing in the streets
Miraculously free from fear.

No. The story went too far.
For even now, at night, safe
And secret under blankets, I know
The fabulist was wrong, when something
Hideous and familiar appears,
Parting the mists and coming towards me.

They still recall the time
When they made the formal garden
Next to the wall of the jungle,
Separated only by a river.
They remember how the children
Would stand and look across

As if something across
There made them see the garden
Differently. Or perhaps the jungle
Smell on the warm river
Awakened something in the children
Before its usual time.

Whatever it was, that time
The children disappeared from the garden,
Footprints led to the river
And a break in the wall of the jungle.
They thought of going across
But held back in case the children

Should return another way, as children
Do, and find them gone in the jungle.
They waited some time
Then left and went back across
The land, away from the river.
What could they do in the garden

But sit and think of the garden
As it had been with the children?
They found a new house by a new river
And in the garden there grew thyme
And forget-me-nots. Across
The country the spreading jungle

Covered the formal garden. Jungle
Creatures prowled where the children
Used to play, crying across
The land as they had in the time
Before they built the garden
And pushed the jungle back over the river.

Now the old ones sit quietly, as across time
Their minds wheel back over garden and river,
Deep into the jungle, seeking their children.

## WINTER SONG

Cold and in the winter weather
Comfort is denied
Doors are fast but still the weather
Rages inside

Security becomes survival
Timbers creak and stir
Between our lives and something evil
A bulging door

Tired and in the greyest weather
Cold savaging the bone
Nightly nightly we grow weaker
And our blood runs thin

Enduring in the steady weather
In the snow's long falling
We wait for rescue — a sudden thaw
Or voices calling

Their bright colours have faded.
One by one they have
Been refined by the years
Until they are no more
Than curious and mingled
Scents, caught only faintly
Yet known for what they are.

Farewell to all of them,
Half-forgotten, but deeply
Part of me, like those flowers
Of a country childhood —
Colesfoot, centaury, loosestrife —
Whose names come back from where
No winters were, nor thorns.

*from* The Barbarian File (1974)

PREDICTION

You said
what will it be like
when we are old
and I told you
how we would sit
in sun and music
under trees
and speak of how
things were when
everything was new
and in its place

I said
we would speak
of how long ago
we stood at night
laughing and crying
and tried to catch
the moon in a net

I told you these things
and you smiled and
pretended you didn't know
that all the time
behind my smile
I was thinking of
how it will be
when the moon is gone
when we are alone
when we are nothing
but clothes and bone

LOVE POEM

An arm
deep
in water
bends
and shines
white
in green
trembles
away its
solidness.

So I
with you
in this strange
greenness
bend and
alter

released
from old
forms
changing
suddenly
into new.

All summer he scans the high ledges for what might move.

Grizzly, wolverine, eagle, wolf are of no interest to him.

Not seeing cougar makes them bigger.

Knowing he has been watched by cougar makes him smaller.

The small head and the huge back legs fascinate him.

He is possessed by cougar.

It's always those who don't want to who see cougar.

Back home he pads lightly on springy soles.

He jumps the long stairs in two bounds.

At his mirror he snarls and hisses baring long teeth.

Imperceptibly his nails grow longer.

More and more these days
old voices and places
turn inside his head.
He looks forward less.

Once he had
a kingdom where the land
met the sea and he ran
in it and starfish dripped in
his hands and he caught great
dark red crabs.

Above him contrails
and soft gunfire in the high
clouds and sometimes bombs
fell near him and his brother.

He found shells of white
by the sea and silver shells
from the plane which one
night nearly killed him.

His children in the city
should know about this
and he will tell them when
they wake afraid of all the noises
how he would wait for the tide
to uncover its small brittle
things but more especially
he will tell them how he waited
most patiently for his father
in strange blue clothes
to come home.

*from* **The Upper Hand** (1981)

DISUSED AIRFIELD

It would be easier to make sense of this
with a movie camera and tape recorder.
The camera would pan slowly, lingering
over the fields, the burst concrete

of the disposal bays, purple with willow-herb,
the still solid foundations of Nissen huts,
to the shell of the control tower,
windowless, grey, standing on a ruined apron.

At that point the recorder would start
with a faint hint of excited voices,
and the film would slowly dissolve
until the set was new again, in 1942,

aircrew chatting over pints of beer,
mechanics in fatigues working on engines,
figures in the tower talking into radios,
Bedford trucks moving around the perimeter.

All would be movement and purpose.
Cut to local village pub. Cut to bombs
on low trolleys pulled by tractors.
Cut to old men and young women

looking suddenly upward in the streets
as twilight draws the first bombers,
climbing hard, fighting for their element.
The finest hour everything would say.

Today I stand here alone,
my eyes panning across sluggish cows
deep in meadowsweet and nettles.
No dissolve. The voices do not come.

And yet, suddenly, how clear my father's
face, his cap, his blue uniform.
I stay for hours, my only tribute,
grounded in the airborne song of birds.

## THE FIELD

That's where
I saw the Lysander crash,
I tell my son,
when I was about your age.
It came straight down
when I was playing.
There were two men in it,
both killed.

But it's flat, he says,
just a flat field.
Where's the hole?

I drive on
hunched tightly around
that scarred place inside me
I can never show him.

TO A GERMAN PILOT
(for Heidi)

I see you later, complacent with a cigar,
an executive in some booming modern business,
occasionally telling war stories over schnapps,
laughing as you show photos of yourself
on the cockpit steps of the black Junkers 88,

but then I may be wrong, and you are lying,
a mess of bone and leather, in a weed-covered
fuselage deep under the North Sea,
or propping up one of those identical
white crosses in a war cemetery.

I know I shouldn't care any more the way
I did then, in 1945, crouching under
the steel dining-room table with my mother
and baby brother, blankets over our heads,
hearing the sky exploding over the house.

My hate went up like tracers at you then.
You crippled Ferdie Freeman with a cannon shell
as he was slow getting to his shelter.
Two passes up and down a harmless
street no more than a hundred feet up.

We were shown some unexploded shells
the next day, silver and red, and told
not to touch any we found. You bastard.
Were you one of the carefree ones, knights of the air,
in a yellow scarf, singing *Wir fahren gegen England?*

You hit no military target that night
but your mission accomplished something
if only that a hundred people would never be
the same. I still dream of you and your black plane.
I dream of the world ending in noise and flame.

Rooks and pigeons have it now
And the rain from the high moors
Which followed us down the valley.
It's the size astonishes, and the quiet,

Out in this remoteness. No guidebook
or photograph prepared us for it,
Suggested this immensity.
Time and weather have been cruel

To the great nave, but still the arches
Soar and amaze. Midwinter.
We are alone on the tended grass
Under the dripping stone,

But suddenly we know we are standing
On generations of the dead, men of prayer
And singing, lying all around
Their massive altered headstone.

Bareheaded we remain among them
In the bird-noise and the drizzle
As time's circle draws us in,
And from the stone there comes

A faint persistent music,
Elusive, half-familiar, celebratory,
As the blowing rain, soft and fine,
Drifts over us like shrouds.

On a mild day, under sun, the moor
Is static and the sea like a postcard,
Too posed, too perfect.

Days like this are better, the November
Sea lost in the weather, clouds falling
Low and thick off Hay Tor,

The trees cold against the grey stone.
The grass thrashes. If it were longer the graves
Would be drowned, lost,

But it is right in this high place,
Right that it should be left alone
To grow and move.

With my mother I stand, cold, northern,
A foreigner in all this Devon wind,
Yet comfortable, at home

Here where a long convergence has ended.
Taking her hand I am proud and tall,
Defined sharply.

High up here, high and strong, I am his first-born,
And what if I am crying as I feel
The day, the wind, the clouds,

Our unspoken hopes, our immense memories
Narrowed and contained by the words at our feet:
*Stephen Wiseman 1907–1971*

FILEY BRIG, 1975

Back again
under these cliffs.

The sea stretches
tight and grey as canvas
out to a cold curved horizon.
My children wade the pools
searching for crabs
and my mind lets go
and for a moment
I am back thirty years
a child in these same pools
free and running
with the long tides
in the bright weather.

Triumphant, my son
holds up a crab
his face alight,
wanting my praise.

AT THE POOL

Not many even dared to start the climb,
Because it meant dodging the sad old lame
Attendant who never let kids up there.

Forty-two feet I think they said it was,
Into fifteen feet of unheated seawater,
And because of the war they'd taken the railings away

On the steps and at the top. But those were glory
Days — 1946, and the military
Band playing 'Nights of Gladness' — and I was up

There alone before I knew it, scared
Shitless, my friends signalling it was clear,
And I jumped, I jumped. That smack of soles and palms!

From the café and terraces above the pool
A round of cheerful applause from onlookers
And I was a hero. I tell my wife all this.

Today, thirty-eight, sitting on that same
Terrace drinking tea, trying to keep
My children from drawing attention to themselves,

I watch the pool like a hawk, praying
That no sodding little wanker will try
To show off by going up those steps.

## ON A PAINTING BY L.S. LOWRY

Here are the matchstick men in the little square,
Some with canes or matchstick dogs, walking
Or standing in groups. Tiny matchstick children
With iron hoops (for this is not today)
Flit about among the thin dark legs.

They are uncountable, these tiny people,
And featureless, unless you look closely.
Behind them rears their world — gigantic
Square brick factories where they spend their days,
Mean houses in the shadows. Haze. Cobbles.

They are caught in hardness and straight lines,
In a grey pen under smoking northern skies.
So many of them. So poor they seem, yet
How important on this day of freedom,
How their dignity defies the squalid backdrop

As if they were the countless dead come back
To taste the air again, to find old friends, to talk.
We don't ask what they are doing or why they
Are there. It is enough to look at them.
But they ignore us, being so busy, and go about

Their business with a sober dignity
We can't help but be impressed by, and, looking,
We are being drawn into their matchstick world,
Perhaps for ever, and it doesn't matter because
They are so earnest, so utterly believable,

So much like us, our own gathered kind,
That it is right that we should join them there,
Huddling in groups to reassure ourselves,
Talking, gesturing, touching, shuffling,
Moving with them away from the dark narrow

Streets of our past, solid, massed and drab,
On our matchstick legs, in an endless procession
Out of the frame, into the uncertain present,
Where, in case we get too serious, children's
Cries, ringing hoops and dog barks tickle our ears.

Early in the morning they start to gather,
Drawn from their worlds of suffering to this place.
Languages collide and bruise each other
As buses and planes from all Europe and beyond
Arrive and unload their pathetic human freight.
Ash-white children with stick limbs, held by hefty

Sweating fathers, their eyes peering stupidly
From blankets, mingle with the not so bad —
The limpers with sticks and crutches, the half-paralysed,
Those with withered arms or knotted hands,
The deaf, the blind, the dumb, the idiots.
But worst are those in stretchers and wheelchairs,

Lined up as if to start a sprint at a school
Sports day, wincing at the shock of the sun, some
Carrying dying flowers, some working rosaries
With white urgent fingers. What are they doing?
What does it mean, this gathering here each day
Where once somebody said she saw something?

That folk still long to go on pilgrimages?
It's more than that, their faces tell you. They come
All believing that a generous God will choose
Them personally for his special favour,
Will single them out for that one great miracle
They have pinned all their hopes and money to.

Among them pedlars move, selling small phials
Of holy water, postcards, plastic statues.
Some nuns pass, rustling. The best clothes wilt.
But then they push into the shrine itself,
Jostling, shoving, coming close at last
To the end of their journey. They move like a tide.

The air is full of incense and garlic. Confused
They try to keep in line but then order
Is lost as blind compulsion takes them.
Stewards try to hold them back, waving
And shouting, as if such words and gestures now
Could stop this endlessly coming and endlessly going.

*from* **An Ocean of Whispers** (1982)

Yes, I'll write for you
though not many will, I think,
not poets at least.
I probably wouldn't have liked you
but I write because you've been part
of my life for as long as I can remember.
And now you're gone, you who
shaped an enthralled kid's picture
of an America which was never there
but which might have been
and now without you couldn't be.

Thin-faced hero of *Stagecoach,*
*Red River, She Wore a Yellow Ribbon;*
Flying Tiger, Marine, obsessed searcher
through the vastnesses of Monument Valley,
sub-commander, Fighting Seabee;
you and Victor McLaglen punching
each other out in John Ford's green Ireland.
You were everything America wanted
and to the end you kept providing —
the cowboy with the paunch and croaky voice,
the old gunfighter still destroying evil.
They struck a special medal
for you when you were dying.
I winced, but secretly I was glad.

And Bing, ears sticking out,
the childlike mournful face
breaking on cue into a knowing grin.
Lifeline to an age of innocence.
The world's most heard voice they say.
Everyone's favourite priest, holy
yet mischievous. I remember
that great duet with Sinatra,

the timing of your jokes with Hope,
Grace Kelly reaching up for your kiss.
Ease. Panache. Golf was the right game.

Rich men. Arrogant. I don't care.
You helped shape me and I'll remember.
And now goodbye to you both,
dying as the master script intended —
cancer and heart attack —
All-American to the very end.

In a rented Dodge, driving
down Gorge Road in Victoria,
I heard it on the radio.
I thought I had forgotten
you but I was shaken.

You reached me.
Back more than twenty years
you reached me, when that sudden
cruel drive of voice and guitar
scattered the sweetness of violins
stirred rebellion in the blood.
We thought it would all
last forever, I suppose —
Guy Mitchell, Doris Day,
Dinah Shore, Perry Como,
Les Paul, Bing reassuring us
over and over that we were fine,
that things were easy.

You ripped it apart, ripped it
in a way we couldn't believe.
Exploded it.
What you stood for
threatened more than comfort.
I bought all your records,
imitated them with three
chords on an old guitar.

Now I find and play them,
Worn almost to bits,
stained from college parties,

and feel again the power
of being twenty, feel the room
expanding, marvel at it.
I still know all the words.

Scruffy kid, fat rich boy —
you changed all our rhythms,
shook the walls of the world.

THE FIGHTER PLOTTERS
(for Dennis and Tony)

(RAF Chenies 1955–1956)

When we were posted there they laughed at us.
It was the St. Trinian's of radar stations,
They said, rebellious, a place of losers

And lunatics. They were right too. The station
Was supposed to guide fighters to their targets
And see them safely back to base control.

Huge futuristic metal aerials
Turned and nodded in their wired-off field,
We put coloured arrows and counters on tables,

Logged conversations between controllers
And pilots, gave fixes to lost Meteors.
At least that's what they thought we were doing.

Instead, for two now unreal years, we made
The craziest Carry On movie of all time
With a cast of hundreds but no plot or director.

What actors it had! Tom Symes, billet farting
Champion, who did the *Times* crossword
In ten minutes flat. Evil-eyed, sallow,

He told us how he screwed his newest girl
On the Mayor's throne at midnight in a council chamber
They broke into somewhere in south London.

Taffy Wills who stole the CO's Vanguard
And, pissed as arseholes, rolled it in a ditch.
He screamed with laughter when they arrested him.

Big Con — Oh God — envied and admired:
*Flash it, Con! Cor, it's like a baby's arm!*
*Fuckin' 'ell, it's like a young sapling.*

(Con's couplings with Dirty Dot in Bovingdon
Were rehearsed in graphic detail every night.
God only knows how she could take him on.)

Dennis in his own world whistling Mozart
Above the noise from games of nine-card Brag.
Gerry, now in Ethiopia.

And more. And the whole crazy lot of us
on buses, roaring out 'The Good Ship Venus'
And 'She Stood on the Bridge at Midnight' to startled

Hertfordshire at 3 a.m. after night ops.
Even the CO's flies hung wide open
Whenever he bothered to walk about the place.

I think of them and wonder. Where have they flown,
Those who measured out the flights of others
With lines and arrows on screens and huge tables?

What gigantic loops through sunlit skies
Have they made, what stalls and unexpected turns,
What landings in soft fertile domestic fields,

In prisons or institutions? Who has been watching
And controlling them through the tipsy years,
Plotting their direction, strength and speed?

From what deep blacknesses of lost nights
Have they called out in confusion for a fix?
Did anybody sane give them an answer?

## CALGARY 2 A.M.

In spite of the fact that it's twenty below
and winter has gone on for five long months,

in spite of being starved, starved almost to death
for greenness and warmth, flowers and birds,

in spite of the deadness of endless classrooms,
shopping centres, television shows,

in spite of the pains in the gut, the migraines,
the wakings, the palpitations,

in spite of a guilty knowledge of laziness,
of failure to meet some obligations,

in spite of all these things, and more,
I have to report that the moon tonight

is filling the house with a wild blueness,
my children grow, excel, are healthy,

my wife is gentle, there are friends,
and once in a while a poem will come.

In spite of the fact that it's twenty below,
tonight I smile. Summer bursts inside me.

EXPATRIATE
(in memoriam, George Wing)

It still seems strange that you settled down here,
You so English, so polite, among the young farmers
Come off the land to get rich; you, of all people,
In Calgary among the white-hat oil men,
The blue-jeaned tearaways in cowboy boots.

Your eye saw the place for what it is, and
At times, unguarded, your tongue raked flesh off it,
Yet you stayed and we sat in your dining room lined
With silver cups and prizes won for golf,
A calendar of Dorset on the wall.

You never spoke about the war unless
I pushed you when you'd had a gin or two,
And then you'd look away, your kind blue eyes
Full of burning tanks and blood-soaked dunes.
The Military Cross and the rest stayed locked away.

You'd talk about your training, though, and how you
Were in Scarborough when I was five and watching
Soldiers like you there. Trying to drive a tank
And demolishing a fifteen-foot brick wall —
*Couldn't steer the fucker!* So we were close then,

As we were here. Fish out of water some said.
If they knew those mean Billingham back streets
Where you came from. If they knew what scorched your dreams.
If they knew how your courtesy, that special warmth,
Came not from books but machine guns and grenades.

Young girl, old ancestor,
you would never have thought
that this exercise you had to do
would survive and float down
the long generations, would be
so prized, so jealously guarded.

To you it was hours of squinting,
of pricked and clumsy fingers,
scoldings, cold rooms, oil-lamps.
It must have taken weeks
of your life, but it was part,
you would have been firmly told,
of every girl's accomplishments,
if she wanted to marry well, get on,
to be an expert in embroidery.
And so you went through your paces —
the alphabet, upper and lower case,
the numbers up to fourteen,
a religious motto, rhymed and pious,
and an intricate flowered border
in red and green, spaced perfectly,
surrounding, as your final touch,
a cheerful-looking over-large bird
on a tiny symmetrical tree.

*Ann Platts finished this work when seven*
*years and half old at Sproxton School*
*taught by Constance Wollarton*
*April the 28, 1810*

You did it and it's on my wall,
thin as rice paper, some holes,
faded, the gilt frame chipped.
It couldn't stand repair.

So young you were but you've
preserved yourself, created
this humble immortality.

Young girl,
your needle pearls blood inside me.
Old ancestor,
I thank you for reaching to me,
for binding with your bright thread
a family across the centuries.

I am your descendant, Ann,
far away,
useless with my hands.

## ASH TRAY

I have it now,
its tarnished brass plate turned
towards the room, just legible:

*From the teak of HMS* Iron Duke
*Admiral Jellicoe's Flag Ship*
*Jutland 1916*

It was my father's
and I remember it
in the hearth by our coal fire,
its wood sometimes dark,
sometimes golden in the flames.

I don't use it as an ash tray —
I have so little of my father
that it would seem wrong
to add to the marks he left
so casually on it —
but I see him, year after year,
bending from a fireside chair,
finding it without looking,
banging out his pipe,
and because of that
the cork centre is scorched,
cracked, worn down, gouged,
and fire marks stain the teak.

I have it,
its active life over,
as if the flagship from dreadnought
broadsides had turned, pulled
out of line, and battered, holed
and burned, carrying its dead,
limped back through long slow seas
to safe anchorage and its home.

Too far. We've come too far.
The heart needs its woodlands
Or it falters, closes, hardens.
We crawl under a white sky
Remembering leaf mould, woodsmoke,

Birdsong in the mild air.
The heart has need of them
So it can take root, can
Spread, soar and arch, can wind
All round this blighted star.

*from* **Postcards Home: Poems New and Selected** (1988)

MRS. ROWLEY

The old gasbag, we called her. Came on Thursday
Mornings, fat and panting, to the back door,
Ten-thirty to the minute, smiling, eyes
Enormous behind her glasses, hair askew,

And sat at the kitchen table, catching her breath.
Mrs. Rowley from the grocer's shop,
Taking orders from her regulars,
But really out to talk, to share the news.

Took out her black book, fussing for it
In her bag, chatted for twenty minutes
Until, on some unknown cue, she'd lick the purple
Indelible pencil and slowly get to work.

*Same as last week for the tinned fruit, is it,*
*Dear? We've got a new line of puddings in*
*And I thought of you....* All done, she heaved
Her bulk upward, stumped down the back steps

And wheezed happily away, losing herself
In the long streets like a soft giant ghost.
Mrs. Rowley, gasbag, figure of fun
In a child's world, back to her corner shop,

To custard powder, potted meat and spices.
The next morning a huge brown box of food
Would somehow appear at our door, as if from on high,
Fragrant, packed lovingly. Those fat fingers!

Until she stopped coming. One day she just stopped.
Big, gossiping, slow-walking Mrs. Rowley
Came no more to talk, to make the food
Appear without a sound on our white scrubbed steps.

Mrs. Rowley, the gasbag, up, up and up,
Up over the city, high and away, out
Of our lives, past new dark clouds coming in;
Mrs. Rowley sailing, towing her time

Behind her, wheezing not at all as she soared,
Pulling away a world of gentleness,
A world of slowness and great courtesy,
A world where words were spoken and food was there.

THE BELL, BOVINGDON, HERTFORDSHIRE
(for Dennis Hamley)

It's had a facelift to cater to the times.
The dirty wooden furniture is gone,
The walls parade new fashionable colours,

There's soup and quiche and homemade shepherd's pie
At the bar, the old toilets in the cobbled yard,
Reeking of piss and puke, carbolic and worse,

Have been replaced by clean sweet rooms inside.
But it can't disguise itself that easily.
In jackets and ties we eat and look around,

Our thoughts back all those years when this was the place
We came most nights, down the hill from the camp,
The place we staggered back from, singing, lurching,

Being eighteen and learning drink. Here we mixed
Rum and cider, ale and Drambuie, swapped
Dirty jokes, exaggerated our sexual

Encounters, planned glorious golden futures,
Heard each other's hopes, made quick friends
And quicker enemies. The Bell. The Bell.

Then we were never going to get old,
Put on weight, become tied down, depressed.
And now we two sit here again, quietly, —

Family men, tired, hair receding —
Look round, talk of those who sat here once,
Remember all the wild and gentle ones,

Wonder about the meaning of memory.
We toast each other as we were then, a quarter
Century ago, drinking to our lost ghosts,

Drinking goodbye to the thin young men in blue,
Goodbye, too, to the Bell, for it's doubtful we
Shall be back, drinking to this surprising meeting,

To our children, as old now as we were then.
My friend, we're middle-aged and going fast,
Far quicker than these fine old walls and roof

Which just need paint and care to outlast us.
We don't mention what we both know, that up
The hill they've ploughed the camp six feet under.

I hold them. Two postcards so well preserved
That except for slightly faded ink and sepia
Photographs they could have been written
Last year. Both show Abbeville, the first
Franked *Army Post Office, 7 July 1916*;
The other, three days later, simply *The Somme*,
As if it were some holiday resort.
Looking now the first seems hurried, nervous.

*This is a fine cathedral which you can see*
*in the distance. The streets are just as narrow*
*as they look. Dy.*

    The second more relaxed.

*My dear little Nancie,*
*again I am sending you a view of this old town.*
*I am now on my way back from the front*
*line. I got all my men there quite safely.*
*The weather is beautiful but so hot. I have*
*written a long letter to mother. Hope*
*you are doing well and have written me a nice*
*long letter. Love and kisses from Daddy.*

Grandfather, I never knew you. You died early.
I think you could have taught me, steadied me.
God knows what you described in that long letter.
I read the cards again, that calm unshaken
Handwriting, for all you knew your final
Words, and I wonder what they felt when they came
Through the door. A simple wonder of excitement
For the girl, remembered from so far away,
So strong she kept them for sixty-five more years.
For the woman a great rinse of relief from nightmares

Of mortars and barbed wire, from immense terror.
Tears in her room, perhaps, some cleaning, then
A letter back.

Such an ordinary address —
*15 Moore Street, South Shore, Blackpool, England.*

DEAD ANGELS
(for Dave and Honor)

No more showy dancing on heads of pins
Or sunning themselves at ease on sunlit clouds.
No more celestial music in our dreams,
Bending near the earth with harps of gold,
Standing high with trumpets over congregations.
And something else will have to be assigned
To be the guardian of children's souls
And give protection from nightmares or hunger,

For these are dead angels that I look at
In a monastery storeroom where a key
And curiosity have led me. Half-dark,
The air hot and thick, blinds drawn on the sun,
Here, among assorted relics of the years,
Among fly corpses and damaged furniture,
Are four angels in a corner, line astern,
Tilted awkwardly together in the silence.

I'm not surprised the monks didn't smash them.
I couldn't. It would be desecration,
Seeing the blue robes, the Victorian doll
Faces, the white and pink and gold,
The long feathered wings furled right down
Their backs. But see the thick dust coating
The bright blue eyes and caught in the folds
Of feathers. A shock. There's been a great fall here.

These presences should never turn to dust,
Nor be piled up, grounded, silenced, abandoned
In such a place. What monstrous innodation!
Compelled. I move around. In the shadows
The wings seem like deformities, turning them
Suddenly into cruel ugly three-foot birds,
All their softness gone, except in imagination's
Memory. Lilies that fester. I think of Rilke,

And wait for pity to come, to feel compassion,
For this is wrong. These are images of light,
Of higher places, the miraculous. These
Are the singing from other worlds, the poems,
The glory shining around. Demystified, they
Stare unblinking in a clog of dust and cobweb,
Sad forsaken spirits who have filled our books
And paintings, cast gold on our history,

And can never be obsolete, for we all crave
To be spirit, to shuck off the dying animal,
To fly amazed, atheist or believer, in high music,
Transfigured and grateful. We all hate
Our misshapen human entanglements,
Our crude limitations, and look for what
Angels signify — light in darkness, music,
And brightness linking us to something else.

But I wonder if it isn't in some way
Salutary to find places like this
And contemplate how glory turns to dust,
Free flight to helpless immobility.
Perhaps we should all know about dead angels,
Dead dreams, dead music, all the airless rooms
Where lambent hopes end up, and beauty, and see
How far we've fallen from the celestial,

How heavy we are, how mired, how *lumpen*.
I don't know. One last look. They smile their dusty
Doll smiles. The shadows play tricks. A lone fly
Lurches heavily behind a blind. I must leave,
Full of dark obsequies. But then, as I
Step outside, bright birds, blue and white and gold,
Unfurl their wings and swoop and climb in a great
Scattering cloud, their songs pealing and belling

In pure enormous harmonies, not strange
To the heart, and I lift my eyes up high to them,
My spirit soft and open to the summer,
And compassion finally breaks in me for what
Is left behind in that gloomy room of death,
Compassion breaks as if I were released,
And it is wide as all the sky and glorious,
As I stand astonished, half-blinded by the sun.


(St. Peter's Abbey, Saskatchewan)

Their furniture is still in here —
The curious high-backed chairs, old
Mahogany desks for letters home,
Brocade covers, velvet curtains —

And it's easy to see them sitting,
Horses stabled by willing grooms,
Mountain clothes unpacked, laid out,
Ready for a short promenade,

Or with plummy voices ordering
Pink gins before dinner, maids
Wisping past in black dresses
And starched aprons, waiters gliding,

Deferential, well tipped, in awe
Of such intrepid wanderers
Revelling in their history.
What tales to tell of mountains and bears!

And it's still their place. Their ghosts
Sit with rugs on their knees
Looking down the valley. The red
Of the map brought them all this way

To take the healing waters, or feel
The real sublime before they died.
Some came to find remoteness
Or ease old bones. No matter why.

To dream of building this out here,
So far from anything, and then
Transform it into magnificence,
Shows they were special in their way,

That it's too easy to dismiss them,
Those parodies with white moustaches,
Pale ladies in silk and muslin, butlers,
Maids, world-labelled steamer trunks,

Their tough proud ridiculousness.
Today diminishment — loud kids,
Jeans, trinkets, banks of video games —
And I surprise an anger in myself,

Some fierce desire for stylishness,
And I feel, from the wide terraces,
From card tables and smoking rooms,
Flushed, braying, their ghosts approve.

## KENSINGTON GARDENS, MAY 1982

Subdued. Black headlines are staring at us
With news of ships sunk in the Falkland Islands,
Crippled by sudden missiles nothing could stop.
We've come to sit, to find normality.
Short sleeves. Summer dresses. Distant traffic.
Children play or are wheeled by in the sun.
Ducks lead trails of camouflaged offspring,
Seeking bread. A convoy of them glides past
When a gull appears from nowhere, huge, ugly,
Skimming the surface of the green water,
Takes the last duckling and carries it
To a flat stone in the middle of the pond
Where another waits. They hold it down and beak
Its guts and eyes through a desperate downy flutter.
A shrill unbroken scream goes on and on.

Kensington Gardens. The right place for the small
Contentments. Today the headlines and now this.
There's anger in me. The gulls preen on their rock,
Then one takes off again, seeking the convoys.
I leave my paper, its news of war and bodies,
Turn my back, stride quickly away, hearing
Terrible wings, fast wings over water.

How little the dying seem to need —
A drink perhaps, a little food,
A smile, a hand to hold, medication,
A change of clothes, an unspoken
Understanding about what's happening.
You think it would be more, much more,
Something more difficult for us
To help with in this great disruption,
But perhaps it's because as the huge shape
Rears up higher and darker each hour
They are anxious that we should see it too
And try to show us with a hand-squeeze.

We panic to do more for them,
And especially when it's your father,
And his eyes are far away, and your tears
Are all down your face and clothes,
And he doesn't see them now, but smiles
Perhaps, just perhaps, because you're there.
How little he needs. Just love. More love.

*from* **Missing Persons** (1989)

Those dances, films and girls forever linked
With songs, songs and ecstatic fumbling
Round bras and stocking-tops. A tune for them —
'Blue Tango', 'Truly Fair', 'Mockingbird Hill' —
Music for Brenda, Pam, Judy and the others,
Which brings back oh their delicious teenage touch.
Ridiculous at my age to remember
The arms and charms, tender lips, violins
Augmenting the dreams come true, the teardrops,
But they're in me, from singing and whistling
On walks and bike rides, hearing records, absorbing,
Not knowing other poetry then, nor needing to.
And now I've found a lot of them again —
'Auf Wiederseh'n', 'Three Coins in the Fountain',
'It's Magic', 'Memories Are Made of This' —
Thanks to a nostalgic world and some
Assiduous collecting. Lost loves recalled!
I make long tapes and play them in the car,
Those songs which dust the glass of memory.
Some have aged badly, or I have, or both —
Clichés so gross that recognition gasps,
Embarrassed at itself. Some are just flat now
And some inane, like 'I'll forever hold you
the rest of my days', 'Your lips may be near but where
is your heart?' or 'Darlin', you send me',
But at their best they're still sweet and catchy,
Those tunes which filled me comprehensively
With wonder, and the thin mono, the crackles,
Don't matter at all, as through it I can hear,
Familiar, offering rich sustenance,
Les Paul and Mary Ford, Teresa Brewer,
Nat Cole, Jo Stafford, Guy Mitchell, Frankie Laine,
Clooney, Crosby, Doris Day, Sinatra,
And I meet myself and those soft girls again,
All of us pinned down and held in songs.

'The Deadwood Stage', 'The Roving Kind', 'High Noon',
'Vaya Con Dios', 'Hey There!' — absurd to like them still.
But I'm glad to have them, these secret loves,
Need them in the dismal times, for we've all
Paid more than we expected for that doggie
In the window, and we know it when
We listen, and we're all alike — 'All I want
is loving you and music, music, music.'
We know it's true, and then we have to say yes
To that enormous hopeful chord called childhood,
Its stupid innocence, its love-filled magic,
The music of our lives before they hardened.

**TAKING THE WORDS WITH YOU**

(in memoriam, Charles Steele)

Now I've lost whatever words I need.

Fifteen years of knowing you and all
I keep thinking about is the last record you lent
Me so I could tape 'Lodi' and 'Bad
Moon Rising'. It was a habit, a thing between us,
When something went bad, someone got us down,
For one of us to whisper, with a smile,
'Oh Lord, stuck in Lodi again.' Just that.

And now it's just those two stupid goddamned
Songs coming back at me again and again,
Guitar figures so simple and insistent,
The trite words suddenly ice-cold ironies.

So how did it happen, all this? I'm lost.
Why, when we were just travelling together?
I know we both threatened to get out of here
If we could, but now see what you've done —
I turn my back for just one short moment
And you've really gone, found some kind of ride,
And I'm left here, stuck, stuck in Lodi again,
No words, just memories, nothing moving for me,
And, pouring pain, a bad moon on the rise.

I'LL HAVE YOU TO REMEMBER
(K.C., 1928–1988)

*Ken Colyer, trumpeter, guitarist and band-leader, was perhaps the most*
*romantic figure ever to emerge from British jazz. He was also one of the*
*most single-minded, his enthusiasm for the jazz of New Orleans exercising a*
*total domination over his life. During the Fifties he became a cult figure,*
*generating a following smaller but no less intense than those which attached*
*to Bob Dylan or the Beatles.*

— *The Independent,* March 15, 1988

Not rare, these days, the news of another death —
Colleague, writer, student, neighbour, friend
From childhood. Each brings its special kind
Of pain. And now this one, the man I spent half

My student days listening to, it seems,
On record and from ten feet away for hours
At 51 Great Newport Street in London.
New fires started there, heated up my dreams,

Excitement pounding from the low club ceiling
From trombone, clarinet, rhythm and his horn
Lifted, or haunting in a mute. All done
Then. Over in the gloryland the feeling

Of hot youngness, wide whirling skirts up high
Above stocking-tops as the jivers strained inside
The circle of listeners. A pint in the Porcupine
Across the street at the break. Today I'm glad I

Got to hear him again, by chance, two years
Ago and thirty after Studio 51.
He looked good but didn't stand to play. His horn
Brought it all back — the joy and even tears.

So much of my passion came from him. I know
Him deeply, specially. In vocals, his accent,
Part black, part Brooklyn, part English, meant
To sound authentic, was strange — 'When I Grow

Too Old to Dream', or 'The Curse of an Aching Heart' —
And sometimes a quaver and not quite enough
Power bothered me, but I can't hear his 'South'
Or 'Wabash Blues' without forgetting all that

And feeling how big this tear is from my past, without
Knowing, in all the sweat and smoke and being lost
In the ache of the blues, that I learned from him first
What grieved, what fed, what opened up my heart.

MOVEMENTS

(for Alan Hacker)

Spotlights in the recital hall flash
off your red wheelchair, and I see
with surprise that it's fitted with yellow
reflectors on the spokes, like a bike.

The clarinet seems too long
as you hold it down by your legs,
small, arranged tidily together.
Your black shoes, uncreased, shiny.
And you're uncomfortable, shifting
as best you can, easing yourself,
shrugging shoulders, wiping your brow.
You linger over changing the reed.

Such music from the three of you,
and I watch your face, active as a boy's
in the lights, as the music takes you.

The notes pour out, pour and pour
and splash like a waterfall in sun,
yes, water falling in sunlight,
then grow shady and sombre, telling of pain,
until they rise and fly once more
all round the hall, bouncing the ceiling
for joy, belling clear from the walls,
moving, racing, flying high around us
and then inside us, catching our bodies,
and you wouldn't believe it but we
are being held tightly in our chairs
not able to move at all. We're sitting
and watching you running, Alan, running.

1.

If she's still alive, she's eighty-eight this year,
But to me she was old in 1947 —
Grey, deep-lined, worn down from the outside in,
Four foot three, sparrow-framed, humpbacked
From scrubbing all her life. Weighed nothing.
Bones and a voice. Not one tooth in her head —
Scared she'd swallow false ones, wouldn't try them.
The same faded flowered apron for years,
I remember. Knotted crumpled lisle stockings.

Every morning from six to twelve she cleaned
The wooden floors of Woolworth's on Stockport Road,
Then on Tuesday and Thursday afternoons she took
The bus and came to do the cleaning my mother
Couldn't manage in our house. Nineteen years
She came. I wish I had her photograph.

2.

The afternoons Mrs. Kibble came were a kind of punctuation in
the long paragraphs of my growing up, giving shape to the weeks.
I don't remember many of her exact words, for the real
relationship, of course, was between her and my mother. My
mother would always make a big pot of tea in the middle of the
afternoon and the two of them would sit at the kitchen table
and talk. When she began to trust my mother, she started to ask
advice, tell her things — about her husband hitting her, her
children's problems. I only heard a few scraps of this, though as
time went on, I saw the tea breaks getting longer and heard my
mother talking more about our family as well as listening.
Mrs. Kibble's voice was a parrot's squawk, at one loud level, gravelly,
often unclear because of the toothless mouth. Even speaking kindly

she sounded strange, gruff, aggressive. My mother, worried about
patronizing and offending her, gave her seven and six an afternoon
but always something extra like cakes or biscuits she
pretended she'd made too many of. Clothes too. Even, I recall,
my father's RAF greatcoat from the war, and kids' things my
brother and I hadn't quite grown out of. And one of her own
good coats 'for a birthday present'. Once, after a lot of talk
about how it was no good to us and was just taking up space,
a dinner service which we never used, and she took it, finally,
sitting there crying over her tea, quite stunned. 'It'll be the first
time things 'ave matched, like, on our table.' Her husband was often
out of work and the seven of them survived on her six pounds a week
from Woolworth's plus private cleaning money. She said she often
just had a mug of strong tea for dinner because she never got all
that hungry.


3.


During the war her husband was in Africa and she didn't see him
for three years. Her oldest son — 'our 'Enry' — was on the Russian
convoys to Murmansk, out of touch for months at a time.
Two other sons and a daughter were in the army. Only 'our
Lilian' was home with her. Mrs. Kibble waited for them all,
scrubbing Woolworth's floor. 'It were 'ard like, not 'earing nothing,
'oping they was right.' Her making the best of things
gave her something special which I sensed even as a boy.
Somehow it went with the fact that after hundreds of hours
talking to my mother she'd never use first names because that
wouldn't be right to her, and she'd 'do right by people', even
by us kids, sometimes slipping us some rationed chocolate if we
promised never to tell our mother. She must have been exhausted
most of her life; probably didn't know there was anything else
but that deep tiredness. But she endured, needing practically
nothing. 'As long as I drink a pint of tea in me bath every day then
I'll be right.' Five spoonfuls of sugar in it when she could afford it.

4. The Cards

One each summer from the Isle of Man, where, by putting
pennies a week into a holiday saving plan, they had a few days in a
boarding house. And each year a Christmas card bought in
Woolworth's. Now, over two hundred miles away, it's the only way my
mother knows she's alive. Three years ago my mother sent her
a photo of our family.

*20 Forber Crescent, Gorton, Manchester. Dear Mrs. Wiseman*

*I know we don't write between christmasses but had to because of
photo. You've gone very small like me old age I expect the boys
are the same but older. Its nice they come to see you at xmas my
17 grandchildren and great-grandchildren came to see me.
Nice to see them but to tell the truth I was glad when they went
because they gave me the headache but we should think ourselves
lucky because many peoples familys don't come to see them.*

*all the best Mrs. Kibble*

I smiled when I read it, hearing her voice again.

This year, for the first time, there was no card.


5.

They had to fire her from her Woolworth's job
Because she wouldn't go, at sixty-five,
And leave the floors to someone who didn't know them.
For more than forty years she scrubbed and polished
That same wood, and there's a fineness in that, in
Making places better for lives to be lived in,
Shining the world with all her pride and strength.
Forty years of bristles, mops, cloths,
Sweet polishes. On her knees for forty years.

6.

Mrs. Kibble told my mother how she put all her newborn
children next to a loud radio. This was to get them used to the
world's noise so they wouldn't need quiet to sleep. Gave them
whisky if they cried. Many women of the war are special. They
understand waiting, and keep their pride and generosity. I
haven't seen her for twenty-five years now and know little of her life
in that time. I think she has known more about suffering than we
can guess at. She has lived for the small things, the occasional
happinesses, and has known contentments. She has taught me.


7.

Each year she grows bigger
To me, and I start to understand how there
Could be grace in that shrunken graceless body,
Kindness in that rasping shriek, pride
In her using only last names, in doing right.
How little we can know of other people.

My mother's eighty-three now. Small. Weighs nothing.
Each year she talks more about Mrs. Kibble,
Takes out her postcards. 'Poor Mrs. Kibble',
She says, and I watch her struggle back down the years,
See tears threaten for a moment, though
If you said they came from love she'd deny it.
Then she gets up briskly, puts on an apron,
And dusts a bit before making us some tea.

THE FALL AND AFTER
(for Douglas Dunn)

The longest day of 1987. A Sunday.
The beach warm and crowded. The tide out.
And there's a man, I'd guess over eighty,
In a suit, a tie, and polished shoes,
Walking, with a stick, slowly towards the sea.
He comes to eight stone steps leading down,
Begins, trips, pitches right onto the road

Below, landing face first, lying still.
No glasses, thank God, my first startled thought,
Right above him, seeing it all happen
From a third-floor window, no phone there.
People come quickly, touch, then turn him,
Blood pouring from his head, his face
Scuffed and dirty, his suit knee torn out.

His eyes don't focus, seem sightless,
But he moves a little, as if in quiet protest
At being there in the road like that.
Someone runs for a phone, another finds Kleenex
And holds it to his head. They gather round
And for a moment it looks like a big family,
He an elder, hurt and needing help,

Trying to sit up, to not be a nuisance.
Now a woman, about thirty, is sitting in the road,
Bare arms cradling his head to her white blouse,
Lips moving as she talks quietly to him,
And I am suddenly crying, surprised
As always by the way kindness can move us.
At last the ambulance, and then he's gone.

A few stitches and a new suit. But is that all?
I think perhaps he'll never try again
To walk towards the sea on a Sunday afternoon.
And the next day his blood is still there
Though you couldn't tell it from the oil stains,
And people go down the steps and tread on it,
Walking across the road to the beach. So

What will I take from this? Just how he
Plunged forward, as if diving to water,
Knowing how old we get, how bodies fail us,
How people will run to help and do their best,
That we are, somewhere deep down, still gentle,
But, in the end, all we can do is watch,
Say what words we can, and wait until they come.


(St. Andrews, Scotland)

How old, how very old, their hands, and how
Their kind faces are taking on a look
Of slight falling as the years keep deepening them.
Seeing them together, you'd know they were
Connected somehow, though one is bone-thin, one
Rounder, and there's no doubt they're sisters when
They speak, as they do in their eighties, of small things —
Weather, times of buses, who the card's from —
Quite differently from how they used to talk
In days when they were more formidable,
But with the easy knowingness of kin.
It seems they've reached some strange even place
Where they're fixed, secure, more fragile than before,
But gentle with each other, with the world,
And always generous, as seems appropriate.

But I'm wrong to make it sound as if the fires
Are cold in them, this restrained civility
All they have left. No, they are still the sisters
Who shocked their world back then by leaving Blackpool
And going away to university,
The dark one and the golden one, strong
And beautiful — the photographs I have —
Playing tennis for the College, rowing,
Playing hockey, warding off processions
Of flannelled fools. Winners. Recognized.
Rivals in the best way. Married well, though just
The dark one had children, and did things right —
The war, crises, everything. Time passed.
Widowed, off balance, the dark went to the golden.
Today the golden moves towards the dark.

Hair grey, deep in age, they shiver in
The wet west wind. Arthritis swells joints,
Twists them. Angina pills stay at the ready.

Deafness makes the simple talk more simple.
So why do I feel good with them? Feel right?
Caught between them and my own children,
I know so little but feel an ancestry,
Dark and golden, though my hair is brown,
Feel an energy not yet used up
From these two, head-tossing, pretty, young,
Demure on the shadowed grass of College courts,
Straining, golden, on that northern river,
Spring-heeled school girls on Blackpool's miles of sand.

What falls here as snow in Ireland is rain in Africa dust. What
falls is pain. As I enjoy dessert children die lying quietly on their
sides. As I turn the key to start my Honda a bomb goes off in
Beirut. As I press a button in an elevator a missile screams across
water or sand. It's the same moon everywhere peering down. The same
blank-faced bastard moon and I can't do a thing. My watch ticks
like a timer, my feet in snowy boots are bare on hot sand, my freezing
face is covered with flies. I am dying in my thin shell of bones.
Sand and rain and ice scar deep inside me. My wife, my children,
try to hold on to me. Words fly thick and useless round my body,
circling, buzzing, landing in my eyes. As an old man dies a baby
shrieks hungry into the world. How can I make the goodbyes decent
and the welcome warm? The baby's brothers and sisters starve in silence.
The moon stares, fat and full. I am dry. My pen is an empty spoon.

Always they bubble, loose, unexpected,
erupting upwards for light, those images
we had thought forgotten, well tamped.

*The remains of a German pilot killed*
*in the war have been found preserved*
*in marshland near Appledore, Kent.*
*His crashed Messerschmitt was close by.*
*An identity disc indicated he was probably*
*a Lt. Strobel, shot down on September 5, 1940,*
*in the Battle of Britain.*

Right away we want more.
Did he carry photographs
of a woman, children, parents, a house?
Or a well-creased letter — *Mein Liebchen…?*
Such things could help us find comfort,
like the way his plane stayed close to him
in the way of faithful dogs in legend.

The news release does add, tastefully,
*Both the body and the pilot's clothing were*
*said by police to be in a remarkable condition.*
But that's not enough, either,
for such a bizarre resurrection.
We have photographs of old bog-men.

The earth has gathered itself, drawn breath, stirred.
We can't leave this unattended to.
Leutnant Strobel is back among us
and will never be done with us,
demanding, as such intruders do,
some kind of difficult ceremony,
our putting our best words for him
on paper and on stone.

A woman sits and contemplates bright flowers
In a vase. There's sun coming from a window
Behind her, full and mellow, lighting the flowers
And the wall beyond them. She is oblivious
To sun and wall, to our staring, to anything
But the flowers, and we wonder who and what
She is, what she's thinking, why she's let
This room become her one rightful place.
She has gentle features, soft in sunlight.
The room does nothing to answer questions — it's
Neither small nor large, new nor very old.
There are books but the titles can't be read.
Nothing for us but shape and light and the woman
Looking and thinking. We can know no more.
We can't intrude into this delicate
Fragile balance, tense and held, of colour,
However much we want to know her world
And hear her voice. Foolish, we know, such thoughts,
But it's hard to leave, stop looking at her face,
For she might turn and rise and walk away,
Leaving the room intolerably empty,
A loss beyond belief, so precious she is.

Image from Bergman:    a piano keyboard smashed to bits by a rifle-butt.

Image:    women gathered together in a square, their children's photographs round their necks Asking. Every day asking.

Image from Updike:    the mother drunk. The baby deep in bathwater. Her arms trawling uselessly.

Image:    the naked girl, mouth gaping in an unstoppable scream, skin melted off by napalm, running towards anywhere.

Image from Hardy:    three children hanging dead. Two from hooks behind the door. The note: 'Done because we were too menny.'

Image:    hundreds of corpses bulldozed into pits. The way they topple, rubberlike, all mixed up. The sign: 'Arbeit Macht Frei'.

These images are mine.
I have more. You have more.
They are unbearable.
They wear us out.
They do not soften or go away.
They bounce around our skulls when we try to sleep.
They burn our eyes.

What will we do?
How are we to live?

Image from Larkin:    'What will survive of us is love.'

Now maybe there's a clue.
Even if it's only almost true.

STINSFORD, THE HARDY GRAVES
(for Robert Mezey)

Under the massive black-green canopy
Of the yew, so desperate to cover them,
His wife, his heart. And infidelity.
Guilt, too — the long stone silences between them,
The cold erosion of those few good years.

Bright flowers on the grave, old now, wilted,
And 'During Wind and Rain' taps at my mind.
Those elegies for her, for all our loves.
Prowler of churchyards, he'd know why I'm here —
That pull, that being drawn to paradox,

But more it's the greying hair, the dull chimes
Of ageing, the consolation their stones might
Give, making death just a bit less frightening,
Commemoration stronger than all our failures.
Perhaps I think we can finally lie tight,

Out beyond remorse, clustered, apportioned.
Their carved names! (I half expect Reuben and Dewy.)
And he'd know, old tomb-reader, better than anyone,
That I feel the tuneless birds struggling to weave,
Inside my head and round these stones, the weathered

Toughness of a living line of words.

Driving casually over a railway bridge
I look down and they are there, in rows,
Jubilee-class engines waiting to be scrapped.
Filthy, rusting, all their valve-gear removed,
They stand, silent black shells, on this last sideline.

Once in a childhood which hadn't lost its fire
These hulks had made the polished rails sing
As I watched them thunder past me, disappearing
Up to Scotland, up to some glorious
Remote destination past imagining.

It's been long and strange roads that have led me here
To this dismal graveyard, where still
The well-remembered names, turned to irony,
Show clearly on their great ruined sides:
*Invincible, Indomitable, Indefatigable.*

This is the terminus, the end of the bright lines
For the boy who watched them in another country,
Now betrayed by this squalor in the slums,
His memories blackened. Six weeks and they are gone,
Hammered and torched into twisted junk, each one.

## SCHOOL PHOTOGRAPH

It's the way we're posed, so formally, in three
Tiers, the back row standing on hidden benches,
The highmaster in the middle at the front

Flanked by the school captain and vice-captain,
The uniform grey trousers, dark blue blazers,
Not a leg crossed, no ghost of any smile,

Just forty-seven poker faces in front
Of that imposing arch of the main entrance,
That makes me remember how importantly

The prefects' photograph was treated.
It was to be part of tradition, after all,
In spite of blowing hair and the occasional blink.

Many of the names are gone, but I know the faces,
Remember voices, habits. We were seventeen,
An honoured few, selected for our various merits

To wear the prefect's braid around the cap,
A black gown, a silver pin, to have a room
For ping-pong, and the chance, often refused,

To read the lesson in Hall. In return, we guarded
Doors, stopped small boys running in the corridors,
Tried to muffle the shrillness of treble voices.

But how can I take this seriously, knowing them?
Oh I knew them! Behind these near-men's
Faces, so beautifully ranged, were nervous

Foul-mouthed adolescents, bragging self-abusers,
Secret smokers and drinkers, shoplifters, bullies,
A few you kept well away from in the showers,

Most of us more obsessed with sex and pop songs
Than with the dubious implications
Of a school history back to the 1500s.

This dignity is a lie, hiding insecurities,
Laziness, the mean-spirited weaknesses
Which have surely nosed our trails into today,

Into what we are (even though some are now
Famous and honoured) and caused breakdowns,
Divorces, sinister sicknesses, early deaths.

Young hypocrites then? Of course. What else
At seventeen? But that's not everything,
Though it would be easier to leave it there,

For today, deepish in life, I'm realizing
That what the camera saw was right after all,
That for this one moment we had all become

What we had been groomed to be — oh, proud,
Perhaps — and that's preserved and can't be changed.
As for all the other stuff, just look away.

Best forget it now, keep on pretending,
And let tradition, and us, live on in formality,
Admirable, quite perfect in black and white.

How casually we let them go, the friends
From early life. And too often it's for good.
So with these two, since 1927,
But now they're meeting again when they are old
By Exeter Cathedral. Smiles, small cries
Of delight, as they hold on to each other, look
Hard into eyes, all the years to squeeze
Away, lives to connect like the end of a book.

Soon afterwards came word that one had died,
Run over on the road close to her house,
Not nimble, unprepared for sudden speed.
No more meetings. But oh, just once, the sight
Of those two friends, apart for sixty years,
Arms open, trying to run across the Green.

There she is, ready for the concert,
Hair coloured, gelled, half-spiked,
Shiny stone in the pierced nostril,
The group's T-shirt, skin-tight jeans,
Old cracking leather jacket
With names and signs she's drawn on it.
Hear her argue about not coming
Home late. Sulky adolescent whine.

All over the floor of her room
What's left of her — school clothes,
Records, tapes, pop magazines,
A mirror, hair dryer, underwear,
An open copy of Wordsworth's poems.

## AGAINST THE DYING OF THE LIGHT
(for Stephen)

One year old, my son was terrified
Of the moon. Nothing else worried him
And he was famous in the neighbourhood
For never crying however hard he fell.
Scoldings produced nothing but a pout.
But one glimpse of the moon, crescent, full,
In between, and he was lost, racing
For the door, for shelter, arms, bed, dark drapes,
Screaming 'oom oom' and pointing to the sky
As if telling of some portent past belief.

Today he heals, with knowledge, with no fear
At all of disease, of broken minds or bodies,
Living strongly, steadily, under the moon's
Long pulling, busy, reassuring others.
But I nurse a secret hope that down inside him
Is left some of the old madness, some fear
Of the great sailing thing he once submitted to,
Which won't let him escape the wheeling terrors,
But allow him to see more deeply, be more soft,
Reflective, transformed by giant light.

*from* **Remembering Mr. Fox** (1994)

The sadness of late afternoon reflects
In the way they walk, so slowly, arm in arm
Along the shore, and you wonder who'll be next
To pack and fill the little car with cases.
They look more often at the sky, as if harm
Might come from clouds, with wide uncertain faces,

Then quietly walk past the still bright flowerbeds
Towards their rooms, and not towards the sea,
Where earlier, just a week ago, their heads
Would turn without a thought. Some stroll high
Above the deserted beach. Some look for tea
Along the Promenade. The benches by the beds

Of roses are chilly for old blood, and they
Are mostly old, this late in the year, and not
So good at coping with the altering days
As they once were, not certain what to wear,
Or how to pass the time, without much thought.
The sea breeze freshens. There's distant haze

On the horizon, turning the sun more red.
In scores of little hotels there are only
A handful left for dinner, and not much to be said
Now, even quietly, at the table or in the bar,
That hasn't been said a hundred times. They're lonely,
These late people. They're too long, too far

From homes and friends, the garden and the pet.
They're restless. Instead of after-dinner walks,
They go upstairs to bedrooms, sit and look out
At the empty sea, talk about the day
And what they did. Uneasy, they turn door locks.
It gets dark earlier. It's time to be away.

And there's ending in the wind that chases litter
Past the closed arcades, the shuttered ice-cream stalls.
The shop that sold the funny hats shows sweaters
Now. The pool is emptied for the season.
Dew beads the benches. Somewhere the first leaf falls.
It's time. It's time. Those locked in rooms have reason.

Dinner in the old hotel by the sea,
Out of season. And each of us assigned
To our own numbered table. Pink cloths,
Pink curtains, pink walls, a pink satin flower
In a thin vase by the menu. Next to me
A man, by himself, facing the wrong way,
His back to the big windows, the sea, the room,
The other guests. Staring at the wall.

Thick with make-up, watching beadily,
Six women in a row talked to each other
Loudly, flashing rings, queens of the place.

Apprehensive, I introduced myself
To the old man and he half-turned, shook
My hand, and said, 'My name is Fox and I'm
ninety-two. How nice of you to talk to me.'
It was the waitress turned him round, he said,
Because his shaky hand sometimes spilled food
And other guests must never be embarrassed.
Furious, I asked him if he'd like
To face the room, but 'No. I'd better not.
Less trouble staying where I am, I think.'
He'd been there nearly two years, he told me.
'It's quite comfortable really. Just a bit
noisy when the holidaymakers come.'

Over the days I talked to him a lot.
He'd been to Cambridge, played top-class rugby,
Had successful children, near retirement now,
Always wore a suit, had read far more
Than I, loved opera, chamber music, art.
Knew Latin. Spoke French and German well.
At 7 p.m. he beamed when I sat down,
And said, 'Good morning.' Then frowned and asked me

To please forgive his forgetfulness. 'Sometimes
time confuses me.'

On my last day
He shook hands, thanked me for taking time to talk,
And whispered fiercely, 'All the others here
are either stupid or potty and I won't talk
to them,' and he stood as I got up, stood
And looked down and shook his head, and I saw,
Surprised, that he was crying silently.

If I went back there now, what would I see?
Big windows, the grey sea out of season,
Pink everywhere, enough to make you sick,
The parrot-widows clicking jewels and cackling,
And either an empty table with no number,
Or that dear man, alone with all his seasons,
Turned by time, staring through the wall.

THE WHITE DOOR
(for Helen Hughes)

They're private houses now, a slab of four
All joined, red brick, gabled at the ends,
And ugly. Pity. I'd expected more.
This was Dr. Ethel Townsend's 'Jallands',

The place for having babies, on Holderness
Road, busy even then and now a roar
Of trucks and buses in a diesel haze.
The doctor, in the end house of the four,

Was famous in Hull, charged half a guinea
For normal deliveries, had four women there
At once. Over the years, I think, how many
Babies? I'm angry that it isn't better,

Special in some way, now that I've come
So far. I note the sad, moth-eaten hedge,
Black and white painted windows, not handsome,
Net curtains, fancy fretwork on the ledge

Over the doors, a roof of wet grey slate.
Later, I'm told, they named a ward for her.
So here, though at the back and rather late,
Was where the world first saw me. God, how queer

To look at that original white front door,
My first door to the world, my mother proud,
My father smiling. Six steps of fresh air, no more,
To where the taxi waited, a black and loud

Austin with leather seats, ready to take
Me, glorious and swaddled, to Anlaby Park.
I take a photo, and studying it now can just make
Out, next to 'Jallands', unobtrusive, dark,

'Floggit's', a shop with nothing on its shelves —
Small, empty, looks like a bankrupt baker —
And also, discreet and gloomily themselves,
The premises of 'R. Boddy, Undertaker'.

SUITE FOR MY UNCLE

1. At the Door

Not a big room. Single bed, three chairs,
A wardrobe, a dresser with a mirror where
Postcards and other odds and ends are kept.
An old converted house. And there's one picture
On the wall, a small TV with a grey metal
Cabinet, a carved bear from Canada on it,
And someone, me if you like, sitting holding
The thin hand of an old man propped in there.
His right arm is curled motionless as if
Fixed to his chest, his eyes desperate on
My face as I talk loudly to him and try
To understand the babbling sounds he makes,
The crippled words he's been saving up to tell me.
His rage. Those baby sounds.

                              And there's a window
Looking over a sunlit lawn, and, further,
A road and people walking. And one door,
Which after today I know I shall never come
In again, and which he will go through just
Once more, awkwardly. Try, uncle! Try!
I need to take your words with me.

                              I talk
About the car I've rented, my family,
And he nods and says yes sometimes, and he smiles
Sometimes, and he frowns sometimes. The face so gaunt
Now. Oh sweet man, floating away like this.
He speaks my name, starts to ask a question,
But again words crumble and his body twists
In fury as he tries to scream the locked-in out.
(The shell-hole back at Le Cateau. His father.)

I say goodbye, pretend I'll come back soon,
Though I fly the next day and he and I are finished.
Again he digs at my hand and tries to speak,
Knowing, or worse not knowing, as I stand up,
What it is that grips his throat so hard,
That makes him whimper when I reach the door.

2.  On the Beach

Almost too heavy to carry,
your childhood.

The day your father blew his head
apart on that beach, and you just
fifteen looking at him there,
at the dropped shotgun.

Almost too heavy.
It blasted your life apart,
deafening you, paralyzing.
You almost in pieces like the skull.
It took you ten years to tell
your wife what he'd done
and never spoke about it again.

Three years later you had to go
to war. And somewhere in all
that wasteland, in the lunatic
deafening howl and roaring,
as if guided by an evil wind,
or something still unsatisfied,
a rifle bullet found your spine.

You wanted children
but never had any.
I suppose there was no connection
with your twice looking, that young,
straight into the ugly, vicious,
filthy face of death.

You were always gentle.
You were my second father.
And you lived, uncle! You lived!


3. In the Book

Dead now. Dead now, not then. Was it fated,
He must have wondered. Was it luck, all this?
Twenty-five hours he lay in that shell-hole, waited
With no words for someone, anyone, moving

His hand, or thinking he did, blacking out
Among the real corpses until they found
Him. The bullet hit his spine, went about
Six inches up. Exited. A spent round,

Probably, or he'd have died right then.
That crater. Dear Christ, while all his mates walked past.
No wonder he was never easy when
His wife went out, that he could never rest

Happy alone, in case the terrors of the dark
Smothered him again. Dead now. Seventy-one
Years after that bullet left its two neat marks
On his back, left him petrified of alone.

Later, back home, he wrote in the front of a book —
*The 25th Division in France and Flanders* —
Near his signature, thinking I suppose about luck,
'Olim haec meminisse jurabit';

Virgil on a very different war.
The bookmark's at the page which calmly lists
His name and regiment — no room for more.
No room for fear, for darkness, bullets, twists

Of circumstance. That hole. '2nd Lieutenant
H.C. Geipel, 13th Durham Light
Infantry. Wounded in battle' — the scant
Army details — 'at Le Cateau'. His fight.

1918. And now he's dead, old,
After long quiet years. In peace he bought
It, not ignored, not in the abandoned cold,
But warm, thank God. His ashes fine and bright.

'One day it will be a pleasure to look back
On these things and remember them.' Perhaps. I
Think of a shotgun, a rifle, the dark, that book,
The gaping exit wound I feel today.


4. In the Church

I wasn't there.
Had flown back, his strangled voice in my head,
remembering the room and hating it.

The Church received him, gave him
back the dignity he had lost. Rejoiced.

Tall candles at each corner of his coffin,
and on it his priest's cope.
Healed. Important.

Hurting, I looked at the Rockies,
mild that day against the western sky.

Just one small wreath by the cope.
Eucharist — more formal than he had used
but that elevation into high words was right
and special. Ripped from us, but brought back
for this tribute.

My mother wore a brooch I'd given her,
had thought through all her grief and fluster
that I should be there somehow.
I'd bought it so casually. And she so old.

Sixty years a priest in little villages
buried deep in Lincolnshire and Devon.
He needed to live like that.

During the service they read some lines
of a poem I wrote for him years before.
A poem of love and childhood. Of what he was to me.
It made them feel I was there they said.

How wide seas are. How alone the heart.

Perhaps I know better now what poetry's for —
small words pulling, tugging, trying to join us,
words circling round our gatherings and passings.

A strange thing on its table
with all the Brontë tourists around it.
Odd in all the stone.

At the other end of the church the family remains,
shaken by the thumping endless feet
(though Anne's away from this, high,
wind-swept, above the sea in Scarborough).
Over and over. Every day. Feet pounding.

Can the God of Haworth be merciful?
Snap. Snap. Lives. Branches. A family tree.
Why leave prayers here of all places?

The visitors come eagerly, in celebration,
but end up with their pain impaled
on thin twigs for all to see.

The children, dutiful, dictated to,
are unworrying — *To Jesus, please
look after my family, love Nicholas* —
but even they can make you think
of complications, things not understood —
*Dear lord, please help my Auntie
have her baby. Love, Rich XXX*

They're collected, sorted, typed, I found out,
read aloud in the service each Sunday.
Every last one. Then left for four weeks
on the altar, near the famous bones.

The strange and simple disturb. Hint
of violent plots unfinished. Dead novels.
*Please let my son and his wife come through
her ordeal of near rape. His Mum.*
Can Haworth's God give help?

(In the parsonage why had I leaned forward
over the rope to touch the couch
where Emily died? For luck? For pity?)

*Can a blind man get a little light?*
*Sylvie from France.* Her father? A son?
World-wide pain, quiet and desperate,
as the heels crash down over and over
by the bones, boom all round
this gloomy shrine.

*Dear God make that boy better, Love Sabiena*

Not an English tradition, the prayer tree.
This has been here just twelve years
and the local congregation doesn't use it.
Its branches fit into a heavy varnished log.
The church provides the slips of paper.

The dead are stacked and stacked at Haworth.
In 1790 more than forty thousand in the churchyard
and it's not big. How many by now?
Emily's room looked right across the graves.

*Help Jim get better.*

Are their bones moving under the floor?
Are their terrible skulls shouting upward
through the din of the feet
telling us that Jim won't get better?
How could they think otherwise?

Feet pound. Bones shiver. Prayers are spiked.

God, don't ever destroy a family this way
again.

OLD FINGERS, SHINING RINGS
(for Peter and Anne)

While my mother reads I watch her hands,
Rough, arthritic now, turning the pages,
And think I've watched them change for fifty years.
These were girl's hands, learning how to sew,
Lover's hands, delicately sensual,
And a young mother's, gentle, efficient.
The rings, unfussy plain silver, still shine —
A matching pair, the diamond not big —
And I've never seen her without them on, ever.
Sixty years since that wedding ring was put there.
I'm made to think of circles of love and family,
Health, happiness, sickness, long widowhood,
Old age. The way it goes. I watch her sit,
Slowly turning pages, over-used by life.

How hard rings are! How they last! And how soft
And quick to wear, so vulnerable, so
Easily ripped apart, the family.
Yet her rings flash lightning at it all
On curled, twisted fingers, shining and circling
The living, the dear dead. I grieve for the years
She's known, we all have, and the ones to come.
Looking, I want to be harder than the flesh,
Change back these worn hands that played tennis,
Deftly dealt a hand at bridge, buttoned
Baby clothes and stunning evening gowns.
Stupid. But the rings tell me something she knows —
To last as best you can, to be brighter than death is,
To pass round and round what shines of you, always.

# A LETTER, LONG DELAYED, TO DORIS DAY

> *There are some things in a man's heart*
> *that don't show up in a cardiogram.*
> — Doris Day in *I'll See You in my Dreams*

I remember clearly.
It was 'On Moonlight Bay', 1951,
in the enormous plush-seated Regal
which had survived the war's bombs.
My first Hollywood musical, and I fell
so hard for you I sat through it twice.

So bright you were! And how grey
my adolescence in the city.
You gave me things I needed —
colour, hope, the joy of love fulfilled,
a place of happy endings across a sea
of time and place — and I yearned
for you as only the young can do,
watched you over and over, played
your records to bits, dreamed about you.
My secret love! I was furious when I
found out my friends all loved you too.

I hadn't heard the jokes and stories then.
They said you were just the girl next door
— they didn't know the girls in Manchester —
and the one about knowing Doris Day
before she was a virgin. There are rumours,
too, of an affair with Ronald Reagan. That
still hurts. In the real Deadwood, by the real
Calamity Jane's grave, I heard the young tour guide
making fun of the All-American blonde playing
a hard-drinking, hard-fornicating pioneer,
and the tourist crowd dutifully laughed.
I was angry, there in South Dakota;

took photographs of Jane and Hickok's graves.
And now they say you're nutty,
talking to dogs and cats, and out of touch.
I don't care about this. Back then I would
have given everything I owned for just one kiss,
hitchhiked to the Black Hills for a glimpse.
Now I can hear your songs again, clearer
than ever. Watch you on video at home.
I have your photo signed for me with love.

So what then, today, with you and me?
Time does its work, but never
lets us forget the blood's first intensities.
And so I send you not just my vague greetings,
but a boy's love letter so long overdue,
and a huge gratitude for what you gave,
all unknowing, to a young and wanting kid —
music, love, laughter, dancing —
which even in these sour and brittle days
can make him sing, bring back a smile
as well as sadness for what we both once were.

REVELATIONS
(for Deborah Miller)

O what a day for the patisserie
with its cakes and chocolates and all
its coffees and teas and our talk
and what a day with the sun so hot
and you in a ribboned wide straw hat
wearing a summer blouse so cool
and stylish and yes what a day
for fudge cake and ice cream and you
telling me about your graduation dance
on that Mississippi riverboat, and you
should be there now in the scent
of magnolia in that hat and a long dress
holding a bouquet for today's a day
for flowers and you should have
white and yellow armfuls in the sun
or at least one long-stemmed rose,
and the breeze is warm as we walk away
and you have to quickly lift your arm
and hold on to the brim of that fine hat
and through the wide sleeve of your blouse
I marvelling see the whole of your
pale left breast — so natural, so
delicious, so sweet and so warm
the afternoon — and I think we must remember
such things, such warmth, such tastings,
for the cool air will be coming soon
through door and window past your photos
of the riverboat and its sweet orchestra
and into the dark place where the straw
hat will be stored for long months,
so yes a day we just have to notice
for the espresso and the two hours
of our being other people in other places
long ago in other suns and how we tasted

appetite tasted things consumed
(so sweet) and things revealed (so sweet)
and there may never be another afternoon
so good and so lucky and how sad that it
always comes back to time in the end
as it does time after time, but O you
holding your hat in the breeze
and my feeling so unexpectedly
one of life's good fleeting moments
one of its warm gusts of suddenness
and what a day yes really what a day
for leaving time six lines behind!

He thrusts and pants and pants and grunts
To show his depth of feeling
While she lies back and with her eyes
Redecorates the ceiling

CARDS FROM SCARBOROUGH

(for Sally and Ken Hull)

However old the card, the weather's first.
It's always beautiful, glorious, bracing, fresh, misty,
Cold, rainy, but nobody really seems to mind
Because they're nearly all having a good time,
A grand time, a lovely holiday here.
Many are like parodies. There's Mabel,
In 1922, *having a topping*
*time,* Rosie Buttey in 1906
Has *a fearful cold,* Winnie, to her Granny,
Claims to be having a *ripping time* in perfect
Weather in 1928. *You don't*
*half see some stunts* at the bathing pool, writes
Another Winnie, and she is *enjoying herself*
*not half.* Romance is here, of course. Jessie
Tells her friend Miss Ambler *I'm just going*
*to meet HIM. He sent a note.* (Seventy-one
Years ago, that meeting. I hope it went well.)
Ethel informs her mother, before the First War,
That *I think I shall come home engaged,* and some
Woman, no name given, sending a picture
Of Rowntree's Café to a Mr. Hepworth,
Bravely asks *Will you come and have tea with me?*
Nineteen-oh-three that. Pretty daring then.
Annie Travis is exasperated:
*Tell Auntie if she wants some rhubarb to go*
*and help herself.* Clara, in '47,
Has *managed the Innox Milk and Powder but not*
*the crochet book,* and M. wants Mrs. Smilley
To *take up to Mrs. Kirk a shilling tomorrow.*
M. Lazenby, 1908, has to
Ask her mother to post the letter she
Forgot — *if you have not seen it you will*
*find it under the melodeum,*
While N. T. from London frets about the coat

That *should have been sent off*. A. Betts wants
Coal in the fireplace when they get back home,
And wants Mrs. Sandford, of Tog Ing, Huddersfield,
To *ask Clapham to leave 1 pt. of milk.*

There are sad ones, too, from this lovely town,
Not just like Cis's in 1910 — *This is
the worst holiday I have ever had* —
But worse. Edie, distressed, 1915,
*Sorry to tell you we have a good mare laid
dying in the stable, best we have,
Blood Poison has set in she is dying
from Lockjaw she will be dead by morning she
is in agony with Pain,* and Annie tries
To console the bereaved and shattered Isobel,
Come from Dumfries hoping *the sea air will brace*
Because *she dreads the empty house waiting.*
So many people, all come to the sea
Hoping. Some cards puzzle, tantalize.
Nan praises Captain Kelly of Guildford
In 1935 — *Dear Capt. Your powder
was very nice.* Drew Knaggs from Hertfordshire,
A small boy, was *sent off to school in a large taxi,*
As *he's the right sort to go to boarding school.*
(Poor sod — I wonder what he did to deserve it.)
*I am quite looking forward to you now,*
Allows *your true friend Gladys* to Buddy in Wales.
Then there's *I have gone goodbye. H. B. A. M. S.
B. R. S. S. T. W. V. K.*
(If anyone can solve this, let me know.)
In '56, clearly quite disturbed,
Jim sends a message to his friends *The Staff,
Bradford Corporation Cleansing Department,*
Which must have meant a lot to those concerned:

*What a wreck Jones has made of the place. Lots*
*of sad-eyed girls. Good luck to R. R.* Amen.
More grim, early on in the war, *we saw*
*a big convoy go past this morning. With love*
*A. E. Atkins.*
            These cards picture a century
Of the heart's softness, fragments of long stories,
Tiny memorials made to be thrown away.
But they connect us, not just to this place,
But to those who shaped us. We like these people.
*This a.m. I went out intending to have*
*a read in Holbeck Gardens and just as I*
*was going in somebody spoke to me*
*and who do you think it was but Nellie so*
*we had a nice sit down and a talk of course*
*Mrs. M. was there as well, she told*
*me you were coming but she did not think*
*coming so soon....* 1909 that one.
Gardens, sea, delight in other people.
This pile of cards, the pictures of South Bay,
The Spa, the harbour. However faint, or trite,
The old words matter, open up a world.
Like a child's first glimpse of sea. The long slow waves.

Yesterday I left her. Eighty-five,
Small, long-widowed, but tough, so full of years
They seem to spill out from her memory alive.
She talks about the Spa, and it appears

It was a special lovers' place for her
In the twenties, wanting somewhere smart,
But not too smart, to go to, for they were
Not rich. They came on his motorbike. The heart

Could scarcely be inflamed by tea dances,
But as I stand here, I think of how they would walk
On the sand, here in the evening, how their glances
Might have led to the cliff-path seats for talk

And whatever 'dalliance' meant. Shadowed trees
Up above the lights and music — oh whatever
They did I feel them and whisper *please*
To their ghosts to show themselves to me. Never

Since he died so long ago does he feel so near
Or she so lovely. The posh tea dance. Then
What? Did they change clothes somewhere in here
For the motorbike ride home? I'll ask her when

I see her. Or, in the late dark, did they ride
Fast, in suit and dance dress, her arms hard round
Him, head sideways on his back? They would have made
No move towards a hotel, risk being found,

Her home so near, and respectability.
No. They'd roar past the wide and moonlit farms,
Shaking villagers in their beds, the sea
And music in them, dancing, kisses, arms,

And tempted to be fanciful, I see hair
And jacket flying, her dress billowing, the two
Yelling, racing the waltzing moon out there
Past Seamer, flushed, laughing, late, but who

Cared? Here, nothing much has changed since those
Days. The orchestra still plays, though now
For the old, and the tables have no aching rose.
She could tell me more, but as her son, somehow....

Besides, I'd rather feel their two young ghosts.
So young! A whiff of her scent for me alone,
Slow tracks, close together on the sand. All those
Perfect nights I want them to have known.

# SCARBOROUGH BAY

(A photograph, 1886)

Tide in but still there's enough sand
For the hundreds gathered round to hear
The minstrel entertainers, turned out
In smart blazers and rakish top hats.
How people crowd around and smile!
The camera is down among them all.
Looking at the cliff tramway,
The long stretch from the Spa, all flagged
Across the bridge to the Grand Hotel.
Further is out of focus, faint.
It's hot, the parasols tell us,
And all of them wear hats, a bowler
Or shallow ribboned straw. The men
Are mostly in suits, women in long
White frocks. A child in a tied bonnet
Is held high on a shoulder. Some
Don't watch the minstrels but stroll along
The water's edge, or sit and look
Out to sea, and one group, like young
Bennet sisters, are gossiping
And giggling, peeping from their umbrellas.
There's every kind together here.
All dead. Every one of them dead.
Not one still alive from all this crowd,
Though apart from some old steps, now gone,
The setting is today, the buildings
Unchanged, the sand, the Spa, the tram.
All dead, these lively chattering ones.
I hang them on my wall to honour
Them, to help me know them better,
Though why I should do that I don't know.

Never the same now. Can't be.
So many have known him as a fixed
point in their lives, a constant which they
thought would last, never change, ever.
But in some committee room they
didn't care, made their decision,
and Max Jaffa's gone, his orchestra,
after all those changeless seasons
at the Spa, Jaffa in his dark blue blazer
and check trousers, his comfy
reassuring with light classics, dance
tunes, sing-alongs, old favourites.
It wasn't enough for them.
They wanted a new image and hoped
they could attract a younger crowd.
They won't. Not in this old place. Never.

What can be done? I sit and look
down at the empty bandstand by the sea,
the music stands, the sad piano.
The Palm Court Orchestra is gone.
What can the mood be but bittersweet?

This won't do. Moving closer
I quietly whistle 'Lily of Laguna',
'The Dambusters', 'Blue Tango', 'Always',
and I see him smile, move to the beat.
He turns. Takes a final smiling bow.

## CEMETERY NEAR BEISEKER, ALBERTA

Far out there in the blue fields of flax,
the dazzling heaving yellow of the rape,
the iron gate has swung

wide open as if in some kind of welcome.
And July breathes hot on us, too sweet and hot,
as we pass by in this

smothering ether-mask of scorched scents
as heavy as prairie ever gets. No use
leaving cut flowers

here, though some have, and recently. But what
of the residents, lying in this swelter
and stink of beauty,

and lying frozen soon in their hard beds
as the seasons line up to take turns
to enfold and shroud

them so tightly they must surely be astonished
at what this land will do to them?
I think they stare upward

bare-eyed at the weather, stunned by it all,
stupefied, gaping through huge sockets,
jaws sagging open.

PHONE CALLS HOME
(John Kordic, d. 1992)


1.


Out of your mind on steroids and cocaine
you trashed room 205 of the Maxim Motel —
tore off closet doors, ripped up paintings.
You'd come in covered with blood, told them
at the desk you wanted 'sleep, sleep, sleep'.



2.


In 1981 I met you.
You and my son the goalies for the Alberta
soccer team. Both sixteen. And you won it all
that year, the two of you alternating.
A big kid. Seemed older than the others.
Nobody got really close.



3.


You wanted more —
the big time, to burn up the NHL,
but you didn't have the leg speed or the touch
to be the star you were in Juniors and you
became the goon, the heavyweight,
sent off the bench to intimidate and subdue.
You were good at it — not many beat you —
became a household name as fighters do
but your parents were ashamed, watching you
fight on national TV. After games you'd
call home and one coach remembers you crying
each time you talked with your father.
You couldn't please him, never got his praise.
*I didn't recognize my kid,* your mother said.

Not good enough to take regular shifts,
you bounced from club to club and fought.
Caused trouble in the dressing room they say.


4.

Designer body to beat all.
Steroids shot into the butt.
Cocaine shot into the arm.
Booze. Groupies. Fights in clubs.
Engaged to a nude model.
Charged with assaulting her.
No coach could hold you in.
Down to Cape Breton.
One last chance with the Oilers.
Back to your home town.
You'd really built your body.


5.

On the soft grass of the west coast
you and my son encouraged each other,
talked about what each was doing wrong
or right. The coach told me he was lucky
to have two goalies as good as that.


6.

That August night in Quebec City,
it took nine policemen to subdue you.
Scared, they left their guns outside the room.
Nine of them, as you fought Semenko,
Probert, Schultz and Williams in your head.

They got you lashed to a stretcher,
two pairs of handcuffs on you,
and still you fought and kept on fighting.
You died like that in the ambulance,
heaving in rage like some tied-down giant
straining to get at someone, something,
the world that had killed your father, and before you
and he had made peace. In the motel room
forty used syringes, eight vials still full.
The pathologist's report — in twenty years
he'd never found so much cocaine in one body.
You won again. Beat them all.


7.


Edmonton. Home, John. The front pages.
Four hundred at your funeral. All there just for you.
Wire service photographs. Flowers piled
high from all across the country,
from folk you never knew. Somehow you touched
them, made grief and pity well up
in strange places. You'd have been amazed.
All for you, John.
All for you.


8.


A boy, strong and agile at sixteen,
doing stretching exercises with my son,
both laughing, the world ahead of them.
Goalies. Specialists. Not like the others.
I was one too at sixteen. It's a bastard position.

9.

After hearing it, my son calls home, hurting,
remembering that week, that strange bond.
*It only seems a few years ago,* he says,
*1981. He was a hell of a goalie.*
*And at least his name's on the Stanley Cup.*
*Not many can say that.*
For a moment we're silent. Then
he hangs up quickly, and I'm glad.

*from* **Crossing the Salt Flats** (1999)

Those two, how they sailed through my growing up!
Fur coats, cloche hats, much powder on their faces,
Oh, they were stately ones as they passed in review

Arm in arm. Out of place there. Their accents
Were from somewhere far away, somewhere
High and refined where everything was better,

Somewhere they'd come down from to our world.
Miss Nan McCardle. Miss Lucy Anderson.
Why, in their fifties, were they living there

Between us and the Shaws, opposite old Fanny?
No man crossed their threshold all those years,
But we didn't, in those days and with those two,

Consider things we might consider now.
We thought that one of them had lost a husband
Or a fortune. There'd been a tragedy, a fall,

We were sure. So long, so long they were next door,
The house dark and private next to our garden.
Their slow, full-sailed navigation of our street.

We tried to avoid them, for their loftiness
Demanded deference from us, yet they ignored
Polite greetings if they were walking together,

Or rather whispering. They quietened the whole end
Of Scarisbrick Road just by being there.
Not women, ladies. Not ladies. More than that.

One taught music at a girls' high school.
The other stayed home, walked silently to the shops.
Why no posh Daimler or Lea-Francis

At their gate, black, with leather seats?
Why no house out in the leafier suburbs
With maid and gardener? It must have been money.

So quiet those two. But listen. From their house
Some evenings glorious full-blooded piano,
A vast passion washing over the city!

(Then my music lessons. A brass knocker,
Lucy grave at the door, the freezing front room,
Plump grey chairs, dust in the air, flower pictures,

The piano with a gilded metronome.
Always five minutes before Nan's sweeping entrance.
She made me learn the words and sing out loud

As I mangled simple songs from an old book.
'Marjorie's on Starlight, I'm on Jack.
Isn't he a beauty, dear old Jack?

'Marjie, are you ready? Wait till Jack
is steady. Race you to the orchard there
and back. I've won!' I wish I could forget it,

Forget the embarrassment, as full of pop songs,
Girls and football, I croaked out all that drivel.
Fear of her, that house, I suppose that's why

It's stuck. However hard I tried, I failed,
And she told me I was letting my parents down
And I'd never — her horror! — manage 'The Blue Danube',

Never mind 'The Tritsch-Tratsch Polka'. I stopped
After a couple of months but even today
I can hear that withering scorn and the metronome

Ticking the long minutes so slowly away,
Feel the clumsiness of my fingers, hate
Those rich little bastards with their ponies and orchard.

After that it was back to 'Good afternoon',
Though even more frosty than before.) Those two
And their strange voyage through my youth. Long gone

Now, and gone, oh gently, stylishly,
Gone differently from others, gone as if
In waltz time to the clicking golden hand,

Gone, waving together, the warm sudden notes
Of the upright, passionate on summer evenings,
Fading like the flowers in their pictures,

The dust slow-dancing in a shaft of sun.
They were not of our world, no, not heavy enough,
Not ordinary. Gone now, those curious ladies,

And all their sad, closed-up grace, leaving
No trace, no answers. Just a huge deep music
In every corner of the street, the years.

Of all the ghosts who peopled my young life
Why do I ask you back? Ignorable
You were then, at the monthly church dances,
Off in a corner of the hall, no mike,
Your thin grey hair brilliantined shiny,
Just you and your dull, dented, silver sax
Playing melody in front of bass
And drums. Strict-tempo men from before the war,
Monotonously tight your ballroom rhythms,
The quicksteps, foxtrots, waltzes and valetas,
With no vocals or modern licks, though you
Sometimes tried current top-twenty tunes,
Sucking the life from them. The hokey-cokey
And the conga were your idea of cutting loose,
Though we — fourteen or so — paid you no mind
In the hot throbbing of our fevered blood,
Our joys and humiliations. Standing in front
Of your bored rhythm men, you never saw us
Or tapped a foot. Your eyes stayed fixed above
The dancing swirl of kids. Where were you then
As your sax played on and on all through
Those years of my young life? I'd know it now,
Playing our parents' tunes, the ones you knew —
'Harvest Moon', 'Always', 'What'll I Do?'

Nobody introduced you, you had no name —
You or the band. You were just there every time.
Came in two small cars, parked on the street,
And I think you were retired, playing church halls
For beer money, an envelope from the vicar.
Ignorable, I said. So why ask you
Back? Sometimes I watched you packing up,
Lighting smokes, putting on your raincoats,
Carrying the instruments to the cars,
Job done but hardly speaking, though I can't be sure,
Distracted by all the dramas playing round me.

Why ask you back, now that the years have faded
You to a shadow, the way all those become
Who help make things happen, promise nothing,
Don't intrude? Because I can see your face
Up there as you played. It's never left me.
Because life's never been like that again,
So urgent, so important, with that steady
And steadying beat. Because, as I look back
To the little hall with its streamers and balloons,
I dance the last waltz again, ah, lights dimmed,
Hands on a waist, mouth in perfumed hair,
The unbearable soft push of silky hips,
Your sax and all of us struggling so hard
To deal with things like 'My Heart Cries for You'.

Polished maroon and gold, chrome dazzling,
my proudest possession as a teenager,
it was a bike envied by friends, looked at
by strangers, kept immaculate by cloths
soft as clouds. Every spoke was cleaned.
I kept it locked, let nobody ride it.
It was a deep pure passion.

I see you in your school uniform
waiting for me in the shop doorway.
I'd ride the bike, whirring, shining, racing
from my school to yours. I could do it
in four minutes standing on the pedals
strong and manly, but more than that
made my pulse hammer when I saw you there.

Back again today. I had to see.
Forty years on and I walk around.
Part of your school is now the Queen of Hearts
Restaurant, with an outdoor patio
by the main road, near where you waited,
full of loud ones eating and laughing.
Part is Scruffy Murphy's Irish Pub.
Sacrilege. But the doorway's still here
where I used to stop that gleaming bike
in a skid, leap off it, leg over handlebars,
see your smile. White blouse, brown
uniform. Mine was dark blue and grey.

Our walks together, you and I, under trees,
around the lanes, away from the road, near here,
together, together, people left behind,
my blood singing, one arm round you, one on the bike.
What more could I have asked at fifteen?

You taught me how to kiss, how to touch
a hot bare breast. Right where I'm walking now.
Our special song was 'My Resistance Is Low'.
I move on. That demure brown cloth,
the astonishing softnesses beneath it,
and how, turning to you, I didn't even hear
my bike crash down in the dirt, handlebars
twisted, front wheel spinning and spinning
as if it would turn my whole life.

FINISH LINE

*Memories like heroes they never grow old*
        — Eric Bogle, 'Front Row Cowboy'

In the old black-and-white on my wall he's posing,
looking right at the lens, smiling, standing balanced
on the pedals, front wheel turned, facing down the concrete
banking of the track. That in itself is special.
Just the two of us that day, and he was good
to pose like that, world sprint champion, for a shy kid
in school uniform. 1950. He even said he liked
my bike, and let me lift his famous red Raleigh
with one young finger.

1993. Back there. The grandstand's gone where I used
to sit, near the finish line, and the track's crumbled
but is still there, the banking sheer and amazing.
Remnants of painted advertisements for Reynolds Tubing.
I scramble down and walk around the ruined place
like some old actor in a condemned theatre listening
to the dead air. Five thousand for big meets.
A trace of white paint at the finish line. Once
a friend and I sneaked onto the track and rode a lap
but didn't dare attempt that fierce banking. Every week
I was there, met the touring pros, the world's best —
Van Vliet, Derksen, Paterson. Heid, the Frenchman.
Reg was the best by a tire's width. Faster than a car
his last two hundred, legs pumping, bike whipping side to side.

1995. Back again, stupidly sentimental, deciding I'd get
a piece of that pink concrete for my desk. Gone. Gone.
The whole track gone. A university residence where it was.
So what do I do now? Reg would stall and fake, then
swoop off the banking and power past to the finish.
Stand still on the pedals until the other broke.

The muscles on his legs. A quiet smile. The fluent
power of what he was, of what I wanted to be like, what
all those people roared for. It was a place of wonder.
A place for the fastest in the world. Now it's dug under.
Now it's for students who've never heard of Reg Harris
(or the track, the crowds) who'll never know that a man
came here from Canada for a piece of concrete and went
home with nothing but heavy memory come alive.
What I was. What I am. The old dilemma. Trying to balance it.
In the photo he's wearing his World Championship jersey.
He and I, nothing can change us now.

## ON JULIA'S CLOTHES

We were some kind of cousins, you and I,
Though you were younger and your brother was
My friend. You tagged along when we went playing
In the woods or by the lake near your village.
I was around thirteen, come with my mother
To visit this less-known side of the family.
We didn't want to take you with us, got
Annoyed waiting for you to catch us up,
Said nasty things. But you wouldn't leave us.
Two visits. That's all. Julia. I forgot you.

It seems you had some problems, went to see
A shrink, fell hard for him. When he refused you,
Got impatient, sent you away, whatever,
You put your father's shotgun in your mouth.
Your mother found you, her quiet and only daughter.
Saw the walls and ceiling. Saw your clothes.

Just early twenties, and they say you were
Very bright, attractive, not strange at all.

I think of you trailing after us, a silent
Skinny ten-year-old. I remember how
The heavy berries hung in the long hedges,
The lake was a clear deep mirror, and we
Thought you were a nuisance and ignored you,
Little cousin, now quite far removed.

STANDING BY STONES

(for Jean)

1.  Chapel Allerton, Somerset, England

You, my wife, brought to tears trying to read
The leaning stones, wiping the moss off them,
Face to face at last with all these people —

Your great-great-grandfather, his parents,
And theirs. They would have guessed someone would come,
Someone from over there, one day, some Comer

Child or grandchild, for a visit, to see them.
Well over a century. You try to copy
Inscriptions, have me take, in the gloom, photos

For Uncle Joe in Iowa and his kids
And theirs. You said we had to come this year,
So we turned off the motorway, through the water meadows,

Along muddy rutted lanes to this little place.
All your life you've known its name, his story.
I couldn't see the graves but you just walked

Straight from the churchyard gate up to the stones,
Up to your family, as if you knew
Where they were, almost as if they'd called.


2.  Somerset to Iowa (1877)

He left here with his savings in gold coins.
All he had. He would have written, months
Later, to these folks under their stones,
That he'd bought land over in America.
Farley, Iowa. Good land, I bet he bragged.

And you, my wife, have one of those gold coins,
A half-sovereign. From Somerset. From the Comers.
You smile at me in Chapel Allerton,
Your face wet, part of a family packed together
In an ancient, dark and tumbledown graveyard.
Now you come from somewhere real, somewhere
You can talk about, describe.


3. Farley, Iowa

The farm is gone. The Comer farm is gone.
Your mother's brother, Uncle Joe, has sold it.
He's old now and his kids don't want to work it,
Have different lives in towns. He has coins, too,
From Somerset. His grandfather's. We sit for the last
Time in the farm kitchen, driven for days
To get here before he finally moves out,
Summer lightning starting, the way it does here,
The evening air heavy, full of growth.
Joe will move. There's sadness in us all.
And you, my wife, drinking all of this in,
Talking about our children, asking Joe
About the Iowa you left, the people,
The whole big thing that was your life, your childhood.
You used to bike here on the gravel roads
From Cascade for lemonade and ice cream, to see
The barns, the animals. Back in the fifties.
He got to here from Somerset, that man.
Joe says to you that it had to end sometime.


4. Cascade, Iowa (1992)

Standing in the graveyard. You, my wife,
Above the little town where you grew up.

Standing among the stones. A quiet hillside.
Here your parents. You've never seen their graves,
Had to leave straight after the funerals.

Flowers burst here. Open sky. Sweet air.
You read their names, then quickly look away.
Ambrose Leytem. Marie Leytem (née Comer).
Another Comer grave. Another stone
To come to terms with however you can.

We drove up here past the house where you grew up.
Slowly. We had to stop and look. How long
Since that day I met your parents there,
Those evenings on the patio with drinks
Watching fireflies. Certainty and peace

On the edge of town and from half a mile away
Over the fields the sound of Dutzy's pedal
Steel as he rehearsed some country blues,
Filling without strain our long contentment.
Everyone who drove by waved at us.


5.  Deadwood, South Dakota

Driving back we go through South Dakota.
I want to go to Deadwood. Always have.

Buses bring tourists up to Mount Moriah.
More graves up here than houses in the town

And it's still in use. You, my wife. You take
A photograph of me by the famous stones

Of Calamity and Bill. I pose and smile,
Remembering the movies and the myths.
I think of people I could send them to.
But I'm sad. Above all I am sad.


6.  Cascade, Iowa (1962)

And one night, I recall, before a storm,
The air heavy as air can be, bullfrogs
Chortling in the pond, we sat together
On the warm stones behind your white house
(Gone now, like the Comer farm. Quite gone.)
Young and happy, our life ahead, hearing
Slow, sweet, over and over, on and on,
Dutzy's guitar sobbing across the fields
'I Forgot to Remember to Forget'.

(in memoriam, A. Leytem)

Deep in a summer's humid evening
From the great slow river they start to rise
Until they fill the hot air with heavy
Drifting curtains, like smoke. They call them fish-flies,

The locals, resigned to this, and they don't like them,
Though at other times the river is a friend,
A muddy familiar giving them a purpose.
They watch the flies drift in, clouds without end,

Rippling nets of them, not noisy, heading
For shore to plaster themselves, weighty and slow,
Stupid, on the first land they can find,
And soon the little town is covered, though

The people take it calmly, closing windows,
Sealing what they can. The season's plague
Is on them from the depths. Is it just here
Or does this happen downstream too? Some vague

Unease must make them wonder as swarms keep landing,
Form deep carpets on street and roof and window.
They stir and shift. They don't do anything
But desperately fly to be there, as if they know

It's all or nothing, they can't go back. Slow cars
Crunch through them, sliding when they brake,
Wipers furious. Those walking cover their faces,
Take tiny steps, as if on new ice, make

Squishing sounds, shake their feet, and head for home.
A transformation! A blanket over the town!
Distant thunder rumbles from the west.
The light is strange in the cloud come up then down.

Next morning machines will sweep, townsfolk
Tend to houses. Dried and small, the dead
Will soon be gone. A few hours for cleaning up
Then only talk is left, the shake of a head

Over coffee. It's not like trying to cope
With the other things that sometimes rise inside us,
Drift through the parted doors of our dark dreams,
Arrive unbidden from some awful place,

For ours are heavier, wait beneath the surface,
And we're never used to them, poised, threatening
To fly, for they'd rise to cover us, once loosed,
Endless, silent, unstoppable, smothering.


(Dubuque, Iowa)

Depressing, the treeless village. Rows of grey
Houses pouring coal smoke, quiet dull-coated
Old women with string bags around the shops,
A noisy fuming 1950s bus,
A bent man walking, pulled by two slow dogs.
No grace or softness here. No laughter. Smoke.
Two small schools — Catholic and Protestant —
At morning break, pale children playing tag
In concrete playgrounds behind iron railings.
In one a teacher rings a handbell, shouts,
Bullies them into neat and equal lines.
Everything seems forty years adrift
And something feels wrong, strange and out of balance.

I retreat into a graveyard, needing colour,
Drawn by the soft cut grass and fine flowers,
Stroll casually along a row of graves,
Start reading. Then I understand. Stone after
Stone explains it all — the grey village,
The smoke, the old quiet people. I walk and read,
One after another down each perfect row.
*Buried in Whitehill Colliery. Killed in
an accident in Bilston Glen Colliery.
Trapped with his friends in Tunnel 30. Killed.
Buried. Accidentally killed.* The smoke,
Thick incense, rises for them, down far down
Beneath their homes. So many. *Collapsed tunnel.
Killed. Dead underground.* Those houses were theirs,
Those were their relatives I saw — widows,
Children, grandchildren — for some died not long
Ago, though today the pits are closed and slag
Heaps and prettified ruins are all you see.
They've kept the village just the way it was,
As the dead would know it if they all came back,
Grimy, jostling, laughing, wanting their ale.
It wasn't meant, I expect, but any change
Would seem sacrilege to those who are left.

I walk further. A different line of stones.
*Infant son. Infant daughter. Taken in childhood.*
More of these than I think there should be. I flinch
At one with new flowers on it. ( Flowers grow
Better than children in this smoke-grey climate,
I think savagely, remembering my own
Two, born not far from here, coughing their lungs out.
That cold dampness. How far away we took them.)

Quickly turning from those two-foot graves,
I come to sons and husbands *Killed in the Great*
*War. Killed in World War Two.* Tough soldiers I bet.
A lot from here, and this just one of the graveyards.
I walk on slowly, clenched hard. Birdsong mocks.

More miners. More. More stones lovingly tended,
Half a mile or more above the bodies.
It frightens, the thought of so much depth in a tomb,
The way the earth closed up and left just names
Formed here in perfect lines, bells rung for them.
Those old women. The wrecked families. The lives
Inside those houses, offering up coal smoke.
And I come from miners — my father's family.
These deep dead ones would have known about
Shotton in Durham. Somehow my line survived.

Nearly at the gate, thinking I've made it,
When I'm done for by one last stone, unbearable
Because of all the others. I hear it spoken
In soft Scots. *Not goodbye just goodnight dear.*
For miners, babies, soldiers, this last voice —
Simple, maudlin, terrible in its love.

(Midlothian, 1993)

Last drive in Britain, five hours to the airport
On a road much taken, its signs always bringing
Smiles, suggesting richness that I miss,
Things I look for, deep, important to me.
And I've been celebrating my mother's ninetieth.
Fowles' Lyme Regis, the Hardy graves, Golding's
Spire, Austen's tomb, this road has given joy,
Cheered me, seductive as any snow-filled woods.
But today it's not to be borne. I see the signs,
Note some new ones, but feel reduced. Gaunt
Inside, yet full, I'm heavy on the throttle.

*baby rabbits for sale … old people crossing … sheep hurdles …*
*flower festival … public bridleway … pick your own fruit … loose*
*chips … duck race on Sunday … family beer garden … polo next left …*
*free range eggs … whole Scottish kippers … heavy horses … 16th-*
*century farm … lurgishall winery … salty monk hotel … fruit … come in …*

Just a few days ago that other drive,
Starting near the distant gloom of Culloden,
The battlefield ragged grass, boulders, low sky,
A small cairn. Dark frightening desolation,
Not like the tourist glitz of the Custer memorial,
The planted order of those miles of crosses
Tended gently in Europe. My mother
Ninety years old on April the 16th.
Culloden 250 on April the 16th.
Well over a thousand killed in the massacre,
The day after Cumberland's birthday party.
(Artillery. Muskets. Swords. Terrible woundings.)
Then driving past Perth I see the *Dunblane* sign.
March, that was, before my mother's birthday.
Dismayed, belly acid, I slow, confused,
Then drive on southward. Suddenly *Lockerbie*
*1 mile.* In one day. Too much. Signs everywhere,

Pointing. I cross into England. Stop. Worn out.
I have to read to children the next day.

*three cups hotel ... eggs self service ... roman villa ... open ... pedigree*
*Nubian goats ... puddletown ... tolpuddle ... affpuddle ... strawberries ...*
*come in ... fancy bantams for sale ... parking ... animal hotel ... open ...*
*great working of steam engines ... test river ... fruit ... pick your own ...*

Should I have stopped at Dunblane, gone to graves,
Somehow paid tribute? The whole world sent flowers
Which lined the streets and overflowed the town.
Schoolkids in Calgary sent cards and letters there.
The five-year-old faces. One of them — Charlotte Dunn —
Sticks but I don't know why. I had no daughter.
The teacher, too, unable to protect them.
The gods defend her, says Albany, and then
Lear enters with Cordelia dead in his arms.
And PanAm 103, its painted cockpit
On the grass at Lockerbie. Eight years already.
Broken metal raining on the town
Like something from deep in the Old Testament.
Two hundred and seven dead. The sky torn open.
Something has me by the throat, but miles,
Still miles to go along this airport road.

*delicious home cooked meals ... bedding plants ... stables ... donkey*
*sanctuary ... point to point ... baby swans hatching ... the Sussex stud ...*
*friary press ... army firing range ... pick all you want ... watch for red flag ...*

I can't drive fast enough. Do I want the airport
And the flight back to Canada over Scotland,
Or just to get off roads, stop driving this car
And seeing signs? How did I pass so much
death in one day and keep going and keep going?

The sun is full. Birthdays and the dead
Are tense in my mind. Birds sing. Hedgerow scent
Sweetens the car. Flowers. Charlotte Dunn.
Children placing wildflowers on the coffins.

*allhallows girls school ... school fête ... children play free ... children
on road ... beware children ... schoolchildren crossing ... children ...*

Crossing what was once their great sustaining kingdom,
Their children lost to them, unnatural death
All round, Gloucester happens to meet old Lear,
Mind overturned, dressed in coloured flowers.
He wants to kiss his hand. Let me wipe it first,
Lear says. It smells of mortality. Foolish
Fond old men, blind and crazy. The land is deep
With the calling dead. I know. I've passed among them.

There on the local beach at Whitley Bay,
A place he loved before it all went wrong,
His old shotgun blew his head away.

And for his son, just fifteen on that day,
A life believing the whole world had gone wrong
As to the local beach at Whitley Bay

They took him, made him look, and he heard them say
Things which all his life locked up his tongue.
His old shotgun blew his head away,

And they asked his son just what it was could weigh
So heavy, and why his mother took so long
To get to the local beach at Whitley Bay.

They moved the body, led the boy away.
In a room they put him with the corpse. So young,
And his father's shotgun had blown his head away.

She came at last. They buried him next day,
The grave apart, no healing prayers or song,
For suicide was sin, and at Whitley Bay
His old shotgun blew all their lives away.

DEPARTURE GATE

(for Jonathan)

My son expects a sonnet in this book,
He tells me, grinning, as we shake hands. I
Say I don't have one planned, then catch a look
Of my father's face in his — the mouth, the eye —

And watch him stride away, through the big door
Where I can't follow. Oh son, at twenty-four
You don't know how important farewells are,
Or how they bring back things too hard to bear,

Grim things from which we think we can't recover.
Fly safely. I'll write, I promise. I turn away,
Remembering how it was to be that young

And things were always waiting, journeys over,
Not left behind, the way it feels today.
(Dad, since you died each day is tilted wrong.)

HEARING SIRENS
(for David Buxton and Andernach)

Driving by the river in the city,
a woman singing on the car stereo,
dressed as usual in my Calgary skin,

nothing special about any of it,
but then I'm back, for no reason, suddenly
back at a river-bend deep in Europe,

that famous rock on the Rhein, inside my early
pilgrim self at one of the world's special
places, however small I remember thinking

it looked at the time. The voice swims round the car.
What were those words about the place, the ones
we learned at school and mocked — 'Nothing

could be finer than to study Heinrich Heine
in the mor-or-or-ning.' Stupid that I remember.
But what were those words? *Ich weiss nicht was soll*

*es bedeuten/ Daß ich so traurig bin.*[1]
That's *it,* I say aloud. The lines about
the Lorelei, her rock, that place of gawkers

clicking shutters and that young me with his life
ahead, in his pack a brand new sixteen-hole
Hohner harmonica in its polished box.

Car engines, the Bow River, the stereo,
but I'm back there, stuck at that bend of the Rhein,
though why there tonight and not New York, Paris,

---

1. I don't know what it means that I am so sad.

Orkney, the London jazz club, Iowa City,
I don't know. Or women, punts, and a soft
green, willow-rich river where once I played

that Hohner quietly and kissed and drank cold wine.
It's not my choice. That once-me, tanned and eager!
The voice in the car has become achingly soft.

*Ein Märchen aus alten Zeiten* — I recall it
now, I think — *Das kommt mir nicht aus dem Sinn.*[2]
A voice over water, irresistible,

pulling men out of their senses to that rock.
A siren sounds on 14th Street. And then
Another. And the voice is deep and clear

filling the car and my eager puzzled head
and the watery whisper and swish of tires is nothing
but lovely and I'm speeding up now, pushed

or pulled by the years, or something, feeling good
and *traurig,* towards whatever's ahead, waiting,
and this present-me, wiser no doubt than that

young one back across the years, is still
not strong enough. More sirens. And I move forward
with all the others, one after another,

tranced, hearing music, something strong and sweet
and strange I can't guess more about but don't
avoid. Not sensible all this. But how passionate

---

2. A fable from olden days — I can't get it out of my head.

the voices and how dangerous, and I know
somehow that it will take some time
before it stops, before I sort myself out,

before I can turn the wheel and steer for home.

(Lincoln Cathedral)

Enormous, white, high above the city,
this place was their signpost home.

Not much chance, and they knew it.
Fifty-seven thousand RAF bomber crew dead.
Ten thousand planes destroyed. One in three.
I must write something. But who for?
Their wives, girlfriends, parents, children, I think.
Today it's just history for so many, distant
as the Norman Conquest, the Fire of London.

Words. I need to speak. But what can I say
about Dresden, Hamburg, Lübeck, Köln,
that I can or can't say about London,
Hull, Exeter, Coventry? All the shattered places?
They say in Hamburg people just caught fire
in the streets, and I can't say anything.
I think I write for all bodies everywhere.
The dead, rather. Many were never bodies.

The sun through stained-glass windows blinds me.
Says yes and no. Says fire and death. Says peace
and safe return. Says sorry and thanks.
The colours blind me. Blind me
like searchlights.

The choir begins to practise. Young voices
soaring and darting in this enormous tomb,
climbing higher and higher, clear and sweet.

Outside, I hurl words as high as I can,
hard and urgent at the blankness of the same sky
where men threw up, pissed themselves,

created firestorms beyond belief. Died. Died.
One in three.

I look at the sun on the white towers.
The old builders believed in a fiery devil,
created magnificence to spite him,
never thinking they built a pointer
for men's red-rimmed arrival from hell,
their landing heavily on the earth.

# GRANDFATHER, THE SOMME, AN INVOICE

1.

Machine guns were the worst,
sweeping the bare mud in arcs,
though marching forward from the trenches,
bayonets fixed, attracted everything
else they had too. One massacre. Another
massacre. Noise enough to kill.
And you there. But before the subaltern's
whistle sent everyone over the top again
a shell exploded in the trench, blowing
you like paper against the boards,
ending the war for you.
And other things.

2.

I hold an invoice sent to you
ten years after that, the date, everything,
handwritten, copperplate, in pen.
It recently fell out of a book
your daughter gave me.
An impressive heading:
*29/9/26. W. & G. Foyle, Limited.*
*Booksellers, second-hand and new.*
*121–5 Charing Cross Road.*
*Over a million volumes always in stock.*
*Telephone Gerrard 3251 (2 lines).*
It looks good. Has lived on well. Survived.

3.

I try to understand this.
In five months, starting July 1, 1916,
415,000 'British and Empire' soldiers were killed
at the Somme. More than 20,000 the first day alone.

Around 600,000 Germans. More than
half a million others wounded. Wave after wave
they marched towards the wire and died.
Trenches often knee-deep in mud and water.
A few tree-stumps, leafless.
Bodies floating in pools of old craters.
The dead laid in rows or buried where they were.
Only later the precise enormous cemeteries.
Five months, the Somme. A million dead.

4.

Men in their nineties on TV, remembering.
The screams, one said. Men screaming
and nobody could get to them.
Collecting the discs and paybooks from the dead,
said another, carrying them in emptied sandbags.
Men crying like children, said the oldest.
Terrified. Clawing at their faces. Gone mad.
And they remembered writing home
on wet and muddy scraps of paper,
and singing 'Wait Till the Sun Shines, Nellie'
before they went over the top again.
His friend's head blown off next to him
in the trench, said another, still grieving,
seventy-five-year-old tears in his eyes.

5.

You comforted the dying, prayed
over the dead and closed their eyes
before that shell got you.
Your hands on all those faces. Blood. Dirt.

You held services before the attacks
from your Communion set, silver vessels
in a battered carrying box. Wine. Wafers.
An old wooden folding table for an altar.
Rough bass voices roaring hymns
in the desolation of the mud fields,
trying to drown the guns.
The last time many of them would ever sing.
'O God of Battles' was one prayer.
The broken landscape. Open mouths.
Screaming shells. Screaming men. Screams.
Wide desperate eyes. These never left you,
gentle man.

6.

After all that, you hid deep
in the Yorkshire countryside, lost
yourself in the small peace of villages.
The country vicar. Safe now.
*The Rev. E. Rigby, Ganton Vicarage,*
*Ganton, nr. Scarborough,* it says.
Tells us the book you sent for —
*Hearnshaw, Social and Political Ideas.*
*Six and Threepence, postage sixpence.*
*Total Six and Ninepence.*
Not cheap back then, and I wonder
what ideas you were hoping to find
to quiet your mind in that big dark house
in the trees — oh yes, I've been to see it —
in the burble of pigeons, the song of thrushes.
Did living with that wound make you
want to think about why people fight?
Did reading drown out the screaming?
Tell you what is just and politic?

7.

And one remembered a seventeen-year-old
wandering, sobbing, away from his trench.
They led him gently back, then shot him.
Three hundred shot for desertion at the Somme.
Did you have to be there at executions
to pray and comfort? Please not.
Most cracked up in the bombardments,
day and night shelling up to a week.
Screamed. Went quiet. Wandered off like toddlers.
'Lack of moral fibre', the army called it.
Abnormal behaviour for a soldier.

8.

*Telegraphic address Foylibra,*
*Westcent, London.* Technology
humanized by the Latin, not like those
telegraphs in the killing fields.
And that huge shop a family concern —
*Directors W. A. Foyle, G. S. Foyle* —
offering personal attention to customers,
as to a dying man in mud, reaching
for help, for anyone, for you.
*Books purchased — a single volume*
*to a library.* One man in a shell-hole
or scores of bodies laid in rows together.
Sorting bags full of paybooks.
*Over a million volumes always in stock.*
No invoice from the Somme, but you paid
with interest on the instalment plan.
It took years.

9.

I imagine you in Ganton Vicarage,
All the bright birds whistling like bullets,
And you with this book, looking past the pages.
I imagine a shotgun blast by some local,
Blazing away at pigeons, and you shaking.
I doubt if you spoke about the things you'd seen.
You lived so quietly, your daughters say.

10.

Blood. Water. Screaming. Shell-holes. Gas. Death sounds.
Five months of 'the great offensive' underground
Or seeking cover. Five months. A million dead.
And at the end they'd won five miles of mud.

11.

Birds and bullets singing in your head,
shells in trenches, by old village trees,
bodies lying, uniformed or feathered,
twitching in mud or soft grass.
And you trying to clear your dreams
with Hearnshaw's *Social and Political Ideas*,
your dreams where living things kept falling
down and calling for you. All the time,
in Ganton village or the Somme, calling for you.
Back home, for months you wouldn't close
the bedroom windows. Wouldn't be shut in.
Sometimes your wife slept in her winter coat.

12.

My own Foyle's invoice from this year is small,
two colours, fashionably unpunctuated,
its heading — *The World's Greatest Bookshop* —
less stylish than yours. A different world.
*This bill must be produced in the event*
*of any query regarding purchase* —
and the address not quite the same —
*113–119 Charing Cross Road.*
But they've grown, brought in reinforcements.
Now it's *Stock of over five million volumes.*
I was there, by chance, on the seventy-fifth anniversary
of the day they realized what had happened
at the Somme. Fewer than half the 120,000
returned unharmed.
That day they picked up 20,000 books.

13.

I hope the dying learned something from you,
if that is ever possible. I hope
you learned something from this dull red book,
because each year, at your quiet gravestone,
swept by a vicious wind come straight from Europe,
I learn nothing. I reach out. Nothing.
Just loss. Just the silent scream of loss.
A shell, a book, a long-dead wounded grandfather
who never knew me, who didn't last.
*Invoice number R2847.*

The cat had kittens at least three times a year.
We kept one for her milk, then gave it away.
My father killed the others. With some fear
I helped him once. First he took a spade

And dug quickly in the wet black soil
Behind the house, between the clumps of flowers.
Then a cloth bag. He filled the scrubbing pail
With cold tap water. Ignoring all the purrs

He took the three or four that were condemned,
Pulled them from their suckling without a word,
Carried them, blind fur slugs, in one hand
Outside. Face set. Softly they cheeped and stirred

As he dropped them roughly in the bag, spun
It closed, squatted, and with a sigh or cough
Pushed it deep into the water. Said none
Of the things I thought he might, just looked off,

Looked away from the bucket. No sound. No hurry.
Seemed like five minutes before he slopped it out
And shook them down into the hole. 'Bury
Them. Empty the pail,' he said, and left. It hurt.

The Bass Rock out to sea, sunlit white now,
And I think of how it was part of those holidays
After the war, staying in North Berwick

In distant Scotland. That shining reminds me how
We took sightseeing boats, on the calmer days,
Around the Rock, two hours, seeing North Berwick

From the sea, watching the feeding gannets, how
They'd plunge a hundred feet just to amaze
Us as we rocked on the Forth out from North Berwick.

Mad skirl of birds! And that one year, somehow,
My father got permission to land. Long days
Of waiting, swimming in the pool in North Berwick,

And then the Bass Rock jetty, and then how
We climbed, avoiding nests, all in a daze
Of shriek, stink and magic. Back to North Berwick

Triumphant, films used up, and it was how
My father managed it, far beyond my praise,
That I think of now, revisiting North Berwick,

Back here, without a father, in North Berwick,
No pleasure boats in the harbour these run-down days,
And the pool's abandoned. Only the birds dive now.

APRIL ELEGY

(Sam Selvon, d. 1994)


I call my mother on her birthday, the way
I always do. Eighty-eight this time and so

Alive, thank God. I can hear her smile. She may,
She says, for this is morning there, go

To the shops later. We talk about the way
She feels, the way England is, her chance to go

And visit her sister. Family talk. The way
We do. I miss her. I miss others. Go

Back when I can. You went a different way,
Sam, old smiler — this time you were asked to go

Back to Trinidad, famous there now, way
Past time. And you were pleased, you said, to go.

I sometimes met you in the shops here, the way
People meet, and we talked of how it was to go,

After the war, to London, alone, and the way
You survived, the jobs, how you made money go

Further in your long exile. The way
You told it, you'd enjoy yourself and go

Collect people and places there, learn the way
You had to write them, make them speak, go

On giving time to lives, pointing a way.
Why were we both in exile? Why did we go

Walkabout from our roots? We discussed the way
Of the world, journeying, the push to go.

You stop on my mother's birthday — nice the way
You did that, like a writer — more shops to go

To, more good talk untalked, and she, way
Across the ocean, this spring day, will go,

My mother, healthy, eighty-eight, the way
She does, to her shops. But you never said you'd go.

Never told me that, like this, you'd go.

I've been reading Plato, she said.
The willow's fretful curtains
Held us in a private shade.

We felt a long slow heat.
How right, I thought. Plato.
The word so cool, remote.

And I watched her quietly
Watching the calm green water
Slide past us, endlessly,

Silent and deep her eyes.
This tableau, then. We two,
Together inside the tree's

Cave, safe from the world's glare.
But for one long stunned moment
Our shadows outside. There! There!

SOCCER COACH

You've taught them all you can,
practised and practised with them.

Now, at the game, you watch, helpless,
head full of silent curses —

*Shoot the fucking thing!*
*Pass it, you half-witted wanker!*

*For God's sake tackle him*
*you ugly misbegotten little turd!* —

as their sun-tanning parents smile at you,
proud of their twelve-year-olds,

applauding every ridiculous mistake.
And you smile back, smile back, smile back.

Through the shattered gates they pour,
Theorists, post-feminists and more.
Smart new fashions are on their side
And so they spread their banners wide —
Radicalize and feminize now,
Subvert the canon, that sacred cow
Of Dante, Chaucer, Shakespeare, Donne,
Which of course is male oppression,
And, worse, realistic, not avant-garde.
(And sometimes, perhaps, a bit too hard?)
Self-satisfied they bond, and claim
That all is text, a language-game.
Reality and goodness? All
That meaning-stuff is past recall.
Now fiction's just to back up theory
Or promote the cause of certain dreary
Groups of marginals — a solid bet
If little's published on them yet
And there's not much on the Internet.
They triumph, for the frightened men
Dare not oppose with voice or pen.
Othered, or worse, the one who tries,
For to argue is to colonize.
People of colour, Derrida, late Plath,
Cixous, Foucault, the garden path —
The old stuff's wrong politically
And that is what they dare not be.
They take six months to learn the jargon
Of obscurity, then they're far gone
In a neo-speak that's all their own
And the inmates get to run the home.
Sad humanists slink home to write
Their realistic books at night,
Or, if they're male and white, not gay,
To calculate retirement pay.

How do new theories of narrative
Reveal to us how people live?
Or queer theory tell us why
Some lines of poetry make us cry?
To them such questions are passé —
Discredited universality —
And deconstructing works of art
Instead of feeling them is smart.
Such solidarity in rabble,
Sustained by complacent psychobabble!
(Thank God for Updike, Munro, Drabble.)
One thing is sure — if there's a heaven,
These zealots will never be forgiven
For reducing people more and more
And using poetry as a whore.
Prostituting works of art
Does damage to the human heart.
They haven't quite killed that off yet,
But look out, the agenda's set.

To reduce eight full-length books and eighteen new poems to a selection of this length is both interesting and frustrating. The problem of revisions of early poems immediately raises its head, as does the choosing of poems simultaneously representative of a long writing career and of a quality I can still tolerate today. I have revised many of these poems, some in very minor ways and some more comprehensively. The concentration on more recent work seems right, especially as all the books but one are now out of print. I have placed the new and previously uncollected poems at the start of this volume, and, thereafter, the poems are taken from the chronologically ordered individual volumes, although I have changed the order of the poems within each volume.

In 'Cards from Scarborough', all the quotations from the old postcards are completely authentic. I have neither added nor subtracted anything from the excerpts I use, though I have split lines in my poem to conform to the metrical pattern.

The sixteen-hole Hohner referred to in 'Hearing Sirens' was a fine chromatic harmonica, which if bought in Germany could be had for about a third of what it cost when exported to England or Canada. The Heine quotation is translated minimally and colloquially.

With reference to the title poem, 'In John Updike's Room', I stayed at the Marine Hotel in North Berwick, Scotland, in 2000, about eighteen months after he did. The people at Reception went searching in their records and gave me the same room he had been in as I requested after reading his poem in *The New Criterion*. (The poem is now reprinted in Updike's collection *Americana and Other Poems*, Knopf, 2001.)

Poems from the following previously published books are included in
this volume: *Waiting for the Barbarians,* Fiddlehead Poetry Books, 1971;
*The Barbarian File,* Sesame Press, 1974; *The Upper Hand,* Enitharmon
Press (U.K.) and NeWest Press, 1981; *An Ocean of Whispers,* Sono Nis
Press, 1982; *Postcards Home: Poems New and Selected,* Sono Nis Press,
1988; *Missing Persons,* Sono Nis Press, 1989; *Remembering Mr. Fox,*
Sono Nis Press, 1994; *Crossing the Salt Flats,* The Porcupine's Quill,
1999. Most of the poems from these volumes were published or
broadcast, and the editors of the journals, anthologies and radio/TV
programmes are fully acknowledged in the books themselves. My
thanks to them and to the always supportive editors and publishers of
the books.

Since these poems first appeared, versions of some have been
published in *Intersections: Fiction and Poetry from the Banff Centre for
the Arts,* Banff Centre Press, 2000, *Listening with the Ear of the Heart,*
St. Peter's Press, 2003, *A Jetblack Sunrise,* Hodder, 2003, the *Ken Colyer
Trust Newsletter,* 2005, and *In Fine Form: The Anthology of Canadian
Poetry in Form,* Polestar/Raincoast Press, 2005. Versions of some of the
new and previously uncollected poems in this collection have been
published in *Arc, The Centaurian* and *Fabric.* Again my thanks to the
editors of these journals and anthologies.

I owe a great debt to the Leighton Studios at the Banff Centre for
the Arts for their frequent and invaluable hospitality, to the Writing
Colonies at Fort San and St. Peter's in Saskatchewan, and to Mrs. Drue
Heinz for my Hawthornden Fellowship in Scotland. Many of these
poems started life in these fine and unique places.

I am privileged to have had this book so shrewdly edited for the
press by John Metcalf and to have enjoyed his unswerving support. I
am more than grateful to Micheline Maylor for her generous and
perceptive reading of the manuscript. And I am fortunate to see my
poems in such a physically beautiful book. The Porcupine's Quill is
much more than an ordinary literary press.

While selecting and revising these poems, I was made, again,
strongly aware of the debts I owe, not only to those poets whose words
have been constant companions for much of my life, but to the two

early teachers and mentors who started me writing, kept me going, and showed me, by both encouragement and example, what I should aspire to. Their names are Brian Giles and Donald Justice. I owe them almost as much as I owe to my wife, who has, with grace and sacrifice, made it possible for me to write what I have written.

Christopher Wiseman was born and educated in Britain, and after three years writing and teaching at the University of Iowa, and seven years at the University of Strathclyde in Glasgow, he came to Canada in 1969. Since then, he has been at the University of Calgary, where he founded the Creative Writing programme and taught until taking early retirement. His poetry, short fiction, reviews and critical writings have been published and broadcast extensively on both sides of the Atlantic, and he has given hundreds of readings and workshops in Canada and the U.K. Christopher Wiseman's poetry has won two Province of Alberta Poetry Awards, the Poetry Prize from the Writers' Guild of Alberta, and an Alberta Achievement Award for Excellence in the literary arts. He was the first Calgarian to be a member of the League of Canadian Poets, has served on the Board of the Alberta Foundation for the Arts, as founding vice-president and then president of the Writers' Guild of Alberta, as editor and poetry editor of both *ARIEL* and *Dandelion,* and he is a contributing editor of *Books in Canada.* This is his ninth full-length collection of poetry.